STRONG START

Pre-K

STRONG
KIDS™

STRONG KIDS™

Other programs in **Strong Kids**™:
A Social & Emotional Learning Curriculum

Strong Start—Grades K–2:
A Social & Emotional Learning Curriculum

Strong Kids—Grades 3–5:
A Social & Emotional Learning Curriculum

Strong Kids—Grades 6–8:
A Social & Emotional Learning Curriculum

Strong Teens—Grades 9–12:
A Social & Emotional Learning Curriculum

STRONG START Pre-K

A Social & Emotional Learning Curriculum

by

Kenneth W. Merrell, Ph.D.

Sara A. Whitcomb, Ed.M.

and

Danielle M. Parisi, M.S.

University of Oregon
Eugene

Baltimore • London • Sydney

Paul H. Brookes Publishing Co.
Post Office Box 10624
Baltimore, Maryland 21285-0624

www.brookespublishing.com

Library of Congress Cataloging-in-Publication Data

Merrell, Kenneth W.
    Strong start Pre-k : a social & emotional learning curriculum / by Kenneth W. Merrell, Sara A.
    Whitcomb, and Danielle M. Parisi.
        p.   cm. — (Strong kids)
    ISBN-13: 978-1-55766-988-9 (pbk.)
    ISBN-10: 1-55766-988-0 (pbk.)
    1. Affective education.   2. Social learning.   3. Child development.   4. Emotional intelligence.
    5. Education--Social aspects.   I. Whitcomb, Sara A.   II. Parisi, Danielle M.   III. Title.
    LB1072.M477 2009
    370.15'34--dc22   2008036063

British Library Cataloguing in Publication data are available from the British Library.

2013	2012	2011	2010	2009					
10	9	8	7	6	5	4	3	2	1

Contents

Contents of the Accompanying CD-ROM

About the Authors
About This CD-ROM

Lesson 1
Supplement 1.1: About *Strong Start*
Strong Start Bulletin

Lesson 2
Supplement 2.1: Basic Feelings: Happy
Supplement 2.2: Basic Feelings: Sad
Supplement 2.3: Basic Feelings: Afraid
Supplement 2.4: Basic Feelings: Angry
Supplement 2.5: Basic Feelings: Surprised
Supplement 2.6: Basic Feelings: Disgusted
Supplement 2.7: Basic Feelings Cards
Strong Start Bulletin

Lesson 3
Supplement 3.1: Basic Feelings: Happy
Supplement 3.2: Basic Feelings: Sad
Supplement 3.3: Basic Feelings: Afraid
Supplement 3.4: Basic Feelings: Angry
Supplement 3.5: Basic Feelings: Surprised
Supplement 3.6: Basic Feelings: Disgusted
Strong Start Bulletin

Lesson 4
Supplement 4.1: I'm Angry!
Supplement 4.2: Basic Feelings: Angry
Supplement 4.3: The Stop, Count, In, Out Strategy
Supplement 4.4: The Stop, Count, In, Out Strategy: Stop
Supplement 4.5: The Stop, Count, In, Out Strategy: Count
Supplement 4.6: The Stop, Count, In, Out Strategy: In

Supplement 4.7: The Stop, Count, In, Out Strategy: Out
Supplement 4.8: Stop Sign
Strong Start Bulletin

Lesson 5
Supplement 5.1: I'm Happy!
Supplement 5.2: Basic Feelings: Happy
Supplement 5.3: This Is Me When I Am Happy
Strong Start Bulletin

Lesson 6
Supplement 6.1: I'm Worried!
Supplement 6.2: The Stop, Count, In, Out Strategy
Strong Start Bulletin

Lesson 7
Supplement 7.1: Basic Feelings: Happy
Supplement 7.2: Basic Feelings: Sad
Supplement 7.3: Basic Feelings: Afraid
Supplement 7.4: Basic Feelings: Angry
Supplement 7.5: Basic Feelings: Surprised
Supplement 7.6: Basic Feelings: Disgusted
Strong Start Bulletin

Lesson 8
Supplement 8.1: What Does a Good Friend Do?
Strong Start Bulletin

Lesson 9
Supplement 9.1: The Stop, Count, In, Out Strategy
Strong Start Bulletin

Lesson 10
Supplement 10.1: Basic Feelings
Supplement 10.2: The Stop, Count, In, Out Strategy
Supplement 10.3: About *Strong Start*
Strong Start Bulletin

Appendix A
Supplement A.1: *Strong Start* Feelings Bingo
Supplement A.2: Basic Feelings Cards
Supplement A.3: Bingo Spinner

About the Authors

Kenneth W. Merrell, Ph.D., is a professor of school psychology in the Department of Special Education and Clinical Sciences at the University of Oregon. He has served as School Psychology Program Director and Co-director as well as Department Head. Dr. Merrell received his Ph.D. in school psychology from the University of Oregon and held tenured faculty positions at the University of Iowa and Utah State University before returning to the University of Oregon in 2001. In addition to his academic experience, he worked for 3 years as a school psychologist for a public school district and has extensive additional experience in providing psychological services and consultation in schools.

Dr. Merrell's research and scholarly work in social-emotional assessment and intervention in schools has been published widely in the field of school psychology, and he has been recognized in three separate studies as one of the 20 most influential scholars in the field over the past two decades. His peers have acknowledged his impact by electing him a fellow in the American Psychological Association's Division of School Psychology and Society for Clinical Child and Adolescent Psychology. His research studies have been published in *School Psychology Review*, *School Psychology Quarterly*, *Psychology in the Schools*, *Journal of Psychoeducational Assessment*, and elsewhere, and he has been interviewed for articles appearing in popular media, including *U.S. News & World Report*, *Family Circle*, and other national publications.

In addition to authoring more than 85 journal articles, Dr. Merrell has authored eight books and several assessment tools. Currently, Dr. Merrell serves as editor of Guilford Press's influential *Practical Intervention in the Schools* book series and is a member of the editorial advisory board for *School Psychology Review*. He is also a member of the Board of Directors at the Oregon Social Learning Center in Eugene.

Sara A. Whitcomb, Ed.M., received her master's degree from the Harvard Graduate School of Education's Risk and Prevention Program, and she is currently a doctoral candidate in school psychology at the University of Oregon. Ms. Whitcomb collaborates in curriculum development and research efforts with the Oregon Resiliency Project, and she is currently a predoctoral intern at the May Institute in the Boston area. Her professional interests include promoting mental health and positive behavioral support systems in schools and consulting with teachers. Prior to attending the University of Oregon, Ms. Whitcomb spent 6 years as a teacher in special education, kindergarten, and first-grade settings.

Danielle M. Parisi, M.S., is a doctoral candidate in school psychology at the University of Oregon. She received her master's degree in special education from the University of Oregon and her bachelor's degree in psychology from the University of Chicago. Her professional interests include improving academic and social outcomes for students through promotion of systems-level prevention and early intervention efforts. Ms. Parisi has experience in assessment, teaching, planning interventions, and consultation around both individual student and systems-level issues. She has worked in Head Start, preschool, elementary school, and middle school settings.

Foreword

Since the 1990s, there has been an intense national focus on the mental health needs of children and youth. Increasing numbers of school-age youth are experiencing serious stress, anxiety, and depressive disorders. It is currently estimated that approximately 20%–25% of today's youth have mental health conditions that would result in a diagnosable mental disorder, yet only about 20% of these youth will actually gain access to mental health services to address their problems. Furthermore, about 75% of these services will be obtained through the public schools.

It is clear that the ability of traditional mental health systems and their delivery mechanisms to solve this continuing problem is inadequate. We urgently need to find ways to promote and provide quality mental health services that are universal in nature, low cost, feasible, and easily accessible and that provide effective tools.

The development of the field of *social-emotional learning* offers great promise for addressing this set of issues within the context of schooling. This specialty shows that social-emotional learning processes are of parallel importance as academic learning processes and that they can have a powerful impact on both academic and social-emotional outcomes. I regard the Strong Kids™ curriculum (which includes *Strong Start—Pre-K, Strong Start—Grades K–2, Strong Kids—Grades 3–5, Strong Kids—Grades 6–8,* and *Strong Teens—Grades 9–12*) as a model exemplar of effective social-emotional learning practices in teaching critical social-emotional concepts and coping skills, including self-regulation.

The Strong Kids curriculum is *practical, easy to use, low cost,* and *teacher friendly.* Perhaps of equal importance, it fits well into the normal routines of schooling and thus does not disrupt the instructional scope and sequence of most classrooms. This program is evidence based and of proven effectiveness.

The Strong Kids program is also highly flexible in that it targets both universal prevention goals and outcomes and also provides more intensive, targeted procedures for individual students who do not respond well to the program's classwide instructional approach. The Strong Kids curriculum is developmentally sequenced into five levels—pre-K, Grades K–2, Grades 3–5, Grades 6–8, and Grades 9–12—thus covering the full pre-K through 12 age range. The Strong Kids program can also be used as part of a Tier 3, tertiary-level comprehensive intervention program for students with the most severe mental health involvements.

I am impressed with the evidence so far of the Strong Kids program's efficacy. A series of recently completed studies document high levels of consumer satisfaction, social validity, and increases in social-emotional knowledge among students who have been exposed to it.

I strongly recommend this program for use in pre-K through 12 schools to address the social emotional and mental health needs of today's students—many of whom bring serious, unsolved problems with them from outside the school setting, which can powerfully affect their in-school performance and behavior. These problems are not of the schools' making, but educators can play a very important role in addressing and ameliorating their more deleterious effects. I think the Strong Kids curriculum is a seminal contribution to the field in improving our collective ability to intervene and prevent many of these problems.

Hill M. Walker, Ph.D.
Co-director
Institute on Violence and
Destructive Behavior
College of Education
University of Oregon

Introduction and Overview

About *Strong Start—Pre-K*

Strong Kids™: A Social and Emotional Learning Curriculum consists of five brief and practical social and emotional learning (SEL) programs that have been designed for the purpose of promoting the SEL of children in preschool through twelfth grade. The *Strong Start* curriculum includes the first two volumes in the Strong Kids curriculum. The first volume is for children in preschool (or about ages 3–5), and the second is for children in kindergarten through second grade. Because *Strong Start* is designed to be both a prevention and an early intervention program, it has a wide range of applications and may be used effectively with high-functioning, typically developing, or at-risk children as well as children with emotional disturbance. It can be used in a variety of settings.

We designed *Strong Start* to target each of the five pathways to wellness advocated by Cowen (1994), which are discussed later in the chapter. Moreover, we created this curriculum as a companion to the proven *Strong Kids—Grades 3–5*, *Strong Kids—Grades 6–8*, and *Strong Teens* programs, which are based on similar premises as *Strong Start* but were designed for use with older children and adolescents. We view *Strong Start* as a carefully designed SEL program intended to prevent the development of certain mental health problems and promote social and emotional wellness among young children.

Strong Start—Pre-K is not the right program for *all* problems or purposes. We especially targeted emotional and mental health problems (e.g., depression, anxiety, social withdrawal, somatic problems) and the promotion of what we term *social and emotional resiliency and competence* in designing this program: We never intended *Strong Start—Pre-K* (or its companion programs for older children) to be a comprehensive program for preventing school violence or antisocial behavior, even though it may play a role in supporting these aims as part of a comprehensive program of effective behavior support.

In addition, we specifically designed *Strong Start—Pre-K* as a low-cost, low-technology program that can be implemented in a school or related educational setting with minimal professional training and resources. It is not necessary to be a licensed mental health professional in order to learn and implement this curriculum.

The curriculum can also be taught in a self-contained manner within a specific environment and does not require expensive community wrap-around services or mandatory parent training groups. The advantage of this programming approach is that *Strong Start—Pre-K* is brief, efficient, skill-based, portable, and focused.

There are several appropriate settings for use of this curriculum, including, but not limited to, general and special education preschool classrooms, group counseling, and youth treatment facilities that have an educational component. A wide range of professionals may appropriately serve as group leaders or instructors for this curriculum. General and special education teachers, speech-language pathologists, school counselors, social workers, psychologists, early interventionists, and other education or mental health professionals may all serve as effective group leaders.

This curriculum was developed with both time feasibility and ease of implementation as high priorities. Even an exceptionally strong intervention program will never make much of an impact if its time requirements and difficulty of implementation result in few people being able to use it within the time and training constraints of a school system or other youth-serving agency. Thus, the maximum duration of the curriculum is 10 weeks (if lessons are taught once per week), and the expected length of each lesson is approximately 25 minutes.

One of the advantages of the Strong Kids curriculum is that it is designed to support academic skills and to be implemented seamlessly within an instructional program. The skills needed to effectively teach students academic and pre-academic skills are the same skills needed to deliver these curricula effectively. You do not need to be a mental health specialist or therapist to use *Strong Start—Pre-K*. The activities in this curriculum not only promote SEL and resiliency but also support literacy, language development, listening skills, memory skills, and self-expression skills. Our experience in delivering this curriculum in preschool settings has shown that teachers have effectively used the program within their regular curriculum and that mental health professionals can use the curriculum effectively as a "pull-out" program for targeted students.

Strong Start—Pre-K is a highly structured and partially scripted curriculum designed to cover very specific objectives and goals. We developed the objectives and goals for each lesson, as well as the implementation guidelines, based on current research findings in education and psychology, aiming for a prevention and intervention program that is built on a solid base of empirical evidence. Each lesson follows a similar format. The lessons provide optional scripts to aid concept delivery, sample scenarios and examples to better illustrate the concept, and opportunities for guided and independent practice. Group leaders can follow the script and examples directly or modify the lessons to utilize creativity. Each lesson relies heavily on the use of appropriate children's literature, role-playing, drawing or other creative activities, and a handout or letter for parents and families (i.e., the *Strong Start* Bulletin) to help enrich the basic delivery of lesson content.

PROMOTING CHILDREN'S MENTAL HEALTH

The primary mission of preschools has traditionally been viewed as promoting early socialization and the development of pre-academic skills, but there is no question that most educators, parents, and the general public have recently developed higher expectations for preschools. Given that providing children with high-quality preschool experiences may help prevent negative outcomes and may enhance children's later school and social adjustment (Barnett, 1995), it is necessary that professionals and parents further define and support what constitutes quality programming. An expanded preschool agenda is similar to that of primary and secondary schools and includes character education, developing good organizational habits (e.g., cleaning up after oneself), promoting citizenship, developing social and emotional competence, and promoting healthy and productive lifestyles. Commenting on the need for this broader agenda, Greenberg and his colleagues stated

> High-quality education should teach young people to interact in socially skilled and respectful ways; to practice positive, safe, and healthy behaviors; to contribute ethically and responsibly to their peer group, family, school, and community; and to possess basic competencies, work habits, and values as a foundation for meaningful employment and citizenship . . . . We consequently assert that school-based prevention programming—based on coordinated social, emotional, and academic learning—should be fundamental to preschool through high school education. (2003, pp. 466–467)

We agree with this statement. We also propose that teaching children positive social, emotional, and behavioral skills is a critical challenge facing our society in the 21st century. As many researchers, writers, and public officials have noted, changes in the structure of society and families have resulted in an increasing percentage of children and families who are "at risk" for developing a variety of behavioral, social, and mental health problems (e.g., Doll & Lyon, 1998; Farmer & Farmer, 1999). Examples of these social changes include a larger percentage of young children living in poverty than was true in the past few decades and increasing percentages of young children who do not live with or have the support of both of their parents. In addition, young children who are being raised by parents who are under great socioeconomic stress, involved in substance abuse, or have mental health problems are at increased risk because their parents may be unable to provide a stable and consistent family environment.

The numbers of children and youth affected by these problems are surprisingly high. Greenberg, Domitrovich, and Bumbarger (2001) asserted that between 12% and 22% of children and adolescents younger than age 18 experience mental health problems of sufficient severity to be in need of mental health services. These percentages represent a staggering figure of up to one out of every five children and adolescents in some instances. Without question, effective responses to these problems, including mental health prevention and early intervention curricula in educational settings, must occur if these challenges are to be stemmed.

Despite sincere and well-meaning attempts to offer real solutions to the social, emotional, and mental health problems of students in school settings, many of the programs or interventions that have been implemented are simply ineffective. We recognize that educators who work on the front lines of serving children with significant mental health issues are often overworked and not provided with sufficient resources with which to make the impact they desire. Furthermore, some developers and publishers of mental health prevention programs tend to overwhelm educators and clinicians with claims of effectiveness, even when there is little or no supporting evidence. Worse yet are reactionary school policies, such as the perennial "get tough" approaches that are not only ineffective in the long term but contribute to the development of systems that are hostile, aversive, socially toxic, and incompatible with optimal development of academic skills and mental health (Skiba & Peterson, 1999).

Despite these problems and challenges, there is reason for optimism regarding our ability to positively affect the social and emotional health and resiliency of children, even those from very adverse life circumstances. One reason for this optimism is the accumulation of a large body of scientific evidence regarding what has been termed *developmental resilience* (Doll & Lyon, 1998). This notion concerns the ability of individuals to cope successfully with adversity, risk factors, and severe life stress and for young people to develop into competent and happy adults despite these problems.

Central to this notion of developmental resilience is the idea that some characteristics of resilience—the cognitive, behavioral, and affective skills that enable one to cope effectively with adversity—may be systematically taught and learned. Although some aspects of resiliency or developmental hardiness may be innate or biologically based, evidence shows that learning plays a crucial role in developing the ability to cope effectively with problems and challenges. Stated simply, the ability to be resilient and to cope effectively in the face of adverse circumstances and challenges in life is something that can be acquired in great measure through systematic and effective instruction in the critical requisite skills involved.

SOCIAL AND EMOTIONAL LEARNING

Another reason for optimism regarding our ability to positively affect the social and emotional health and resiliency of children is the emerging evidence in the area of SEL (Zins, Bloodworth, Weissberg, & Walberg, 2004). SEL has been defined as systematic, cohesive, and effective instructional programming designed to teach social and emotional skills to children and adolescents, to prevent mental health problems, and to provide effective early intervention for those problems that are beginning to emerge (Greenberg et al., 2003). There are many manifestations of SEL programs, ranging from simple training in social or other life skills to expansive, multipronged efforts to prevent antisocial behavior and conduct problems. Since about the early 1990s, an impressive array of evidence-based SEL programs has been developed and made available for use in education and mental health. These programs vary substantially in mode of instruction, time and resources required, target areas, and cost.

The specific type of SEL program selected will depend on the specific needs and requirements of an institution or community and the competencies and problems that are most important to target, but those efforts that are most successful tend to be implemented in a planned, cohesive manner within a system. Fragmented, uncoordinated efforts seldom produce more than superficial, short-term results. Emory Cowen (1994), a pioneer in the modern science of mental health prevention and wellness promotion, has argued that there are five main pathways to wellness:

1. Forming wholesome early attachments

2. Acquiring age-appropriate competencies

3. Being exposed to settings that favor wellness outcomes

4. Having the empowering sense of being in control of one's fate

5. Coping effectively with stress

It stands to reason then, that for optimal effectiveness and impact, any comprehensive SEL program should address most, if not all, of these critical pathways.

SOCIAL AND EMOTIONAL NEEDS OF PRESCHOOL CHILDREN

The *Strong Start—Pre-K* curriculum is unique because it is an SEL program designed specifically to address the needs of preschool-age children, or from about age 3 through about age 5. Although several very good SEL intervention programs have been developed and made available since the 1980s, very few are focused on the unique needs of this younger age range of students.

To be effective, a curriculum must be designed and implemented to be developmentally appropriate for the students for whom it is intended. For preschool children, there are some unique cognitive, social, and emotional developmental needs that must be considered. Cognitively, almost all children in this age range are *concrete thinkers*, meaning that they have not yet developed the ability to think abstractly or symbolically. They usually have difficulty with tasks that require a great deal of interpersonal insight or self-reflection. In addition, most preschool children have not yet learned to read at all. Therefore, any curriculum designed for this age group must be explicit and somewhat concrete, use examples with which the children are familiar, use repetition and review to help teach mastery of skills, require only minimal reading skills, and be short enough and interesting enough to maintain their attention.

Children in preschool are developing emotionally and experiencing many emotional changes. They experience many feelings and tend to understand the general notion of feelings or emotions, but they usually have a very limited vocabulary of words describing different emotions. For example, most preschool children will understand the concepts of *happy*, *sad*, *angry*, and maybe even *worried*, but they will probably not be able to understand more sophisticated emotional words, such as *thrilled*, *joyful*, *tense*, or *proud*. Some of the critical tasks for children in this age range, in terms of emotional development, include developing a sense of self-control, learning new emotional words, learning that what is "right" or "wrong" may be based on more than just the immediate consequences of the behavior, and learning that how something appears is not always how it is.

Socially, children in preschool are learning how to initiate effective social interactions with other children and how to develop friendships. They are in the process of learning how to engage socially with individuals outside of their family and are often surprised to learn that different families have different social rules and expectations, as well as emotional and behavioral climates. Some of the critical skills during this period include learning to negotiate and compromise, learning to be empathetic or understand the feelings and experiences of another person, learning how to effectively join groups and initiate conversations, and learning appropriate use of humor. Many of the friendships children develop at this age are not lasting, but they tend to be very important in terms of providing a situation in which children can learn the skills required to make friends and to be a good friend to others. Children who fail to acquire the empathy or social skills needed to be successful in making and keeping friends are at risk for a variety of social and emotional problems, ranging from isolation and peer rejection to loneliness, poor self-esteem, and even depression.

In sum, any SEL program designed for use with preschool children must take into account the unique developmental needs of this age group if it is to be effective. The developmental needs that must be considered include cognitive, emotional, and social development, among other issues.

MODEL FOR PREVENTING BEHAVIORAL AND EMOTIONAL PROBLEMS

Educational researchers have adapted a public health prevention model for use in school systems (e.g., Merrell & Buchanan, 2006; U.S. Department of Education, 2004; Walker et al., 1996). We believe that this model (see Figure 1) has great importance for promoting SEL and for school-based promotion of children's mental health in general. Sometimes referred to as the "triangle," this model of prevention and intervention includes service delivery at three levels of prevention: students

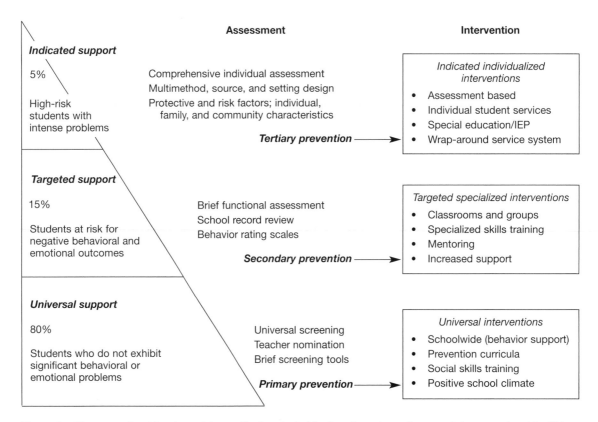

Figure 1. The prevention triangle model, specifically adapted for how to make systems work for assessing, identifying, and serving students with behavioral, social, and emotional problems. (*Key:* IEP, individualized education program.)

who currently are not experiencing learning or social/behavior difficulties (*primary prevention*); students who are considered to be at risk for the development of learning or social/behavior difficulties (*secondary prevention*); and students who currently are experiencing significant learning or social/behavior difficulties (*tertiary prevention*).

We can visualize this model and its three levels of prevention as a triangle. The entire triangle represents all students within a school setting, the majority of whom are not experiencing difficulties (i.e., the bottom portion of the triangle), some of whom are at risk of developing significant problems (i.e., the middle portion), and an even smaller percentage who are currently experiencing significant difficulties (i.e., the top portion). Typical practice is to focus on those students who are at the top of the triangle—those who are currently experiencing significant learning and/or social-emotional difficulties. Practitioners tend to spend the majority of their time and effort providing tertiary prevention (i.e., individualized assessment and intervention services) to these students on a case-by-case basis. These students make up the smallest percentage of the school population, but because of the significance of their problems, they often require the majority of time and resources from school personnel (Walker et al., 1996).

Shifting to a systemwide prevention model requires that we look at the "big picture" by considering the needs of all students, not just those who are referred because they are experiencing significant difficulties. The foundation of a prevention approach is the use of universal interventions (i.e., primary prevention) designed to enhance the delivery of effective instruction and improve school climate to promote academic, social, and behavioral resilience of all students in the school. This idea requires that we begin to move some resources and energy toward those children and adolescents who are not currently experiencing significant difficulties in order to help them acquire skills to reduce the probability that they will eventually rise to the "top of the triangle." More specifically, primary prevention for students who are not currently experiencing learning and/or social/behavior difficulties is accomplished through schoolwide and classwide efforts that involve the consistent use of research-based effective practices, ongoing monitoring of these practices and student outcomes, and staff training and professional development. The goal of primary prevention is to create school and classroom environments that promote student learning and health and decrease the number of students at risk for learning or social/behavior problems.

As important as it is to focus on primary prevention, we also know that not all students respond similarly to these efforts. Thus, it is important to monitor student progress and to assess whether students are at risk (i.e., in need of secondary prevention efforts) or experiencing significant difficulties (i.e., in need of tertiary prevention efforts). Identifying students at risk for learning, social-emotional, and behavior difficulties is an important aspect to comprehensive prevention efforts. For students identified as at risk and in need of secondary prevention efforts, the focus is on the delivery of specialized interventions (often at a small-group level) to prevent the worsening of problems and to prevent the development of more significant concerns. The focus on early identification and early intervention is important.

With respect to mental health and social-emotional problems of children and adolescents, we believe that this prevention model is an ideal way to think about providing SEL programs and other services. Thinking in this way about the challenges we face in promoting social-emotional wellness and mental health among children and adolescents makes these challenges more manageable. Instead of waiting until students have developed severe problems and require extensive time and effort to simply be managed, we can continually focus a portion of our resources on prevention activities that will ultimately reduce the number of students at the top of the triangle.

REFERENCES

Barnett, W.S. (1995). Long-term effects of early childhood programs on cognitive and school outcomes. *The Future of Children: Long-Term Outcomes of Early Childhood Programs, 5*(3), 25–50.

Cowen, E.L. (1994). The enhancement of psychological wellness: Challenges and opportunities. *American Journal of Community Psychology, 22,* 149–179.

Doll, B., & Lyon, M.A. (1998). Risk and resilience: Implications for the delivery of educational and mental health services in schools. *School Psychology Review, 27,* 348–363.

Farmer, E.M.Z., & Farmer, T.W. (1999). The role of schools in outcomes for youth: Implications for children's mental health services research. *Journal of Child and Family Studies, 8,* 377–396.

Greenberg, M., Domitrovich, C., & Bumbarger, B. (2001, March 30). The prevention of mental health disorders in school-age children: Current state of the field. *Prevention and Treatment,* 4. Retrieved November 19, 2005, from http://journals.apa.org/prevention/volume4/pre0040001a.html

Greenberg, M.T., Weissberg, R.P., O'Brien, M.U., Zins, J.E., Fredericks, L., Resnick, H., et al. (2003). Enhancing school-based prevention and youth development through coordinated social, emotional, and academic learning. *American Psychologist, 58,* 466–474.

Merrell, K.W., & Buchanan, R.S. (2006). Intervention selection in school-based practice: Using public health models to enhance systems capacity of schools. *School Psychology Review, 35,* 167–180.

Skiba, R., & Peterson, R. (1999). The dark side of zero tolerance: Can punishment lead to safe schools? *Phi Delta Kappan, 80,* 372–376, 381–382. Retrieved November 19, 2005, from http://www.pdkintl.org/kappan/kcur9910.htm

U.S. Department of Education, OSEP Center on Positive Behavioral Interventions and Supports. (2004). *School-wide PBS.* Retrieved November 19, 2005, from http://www.pbis.org

Walker, H.M., Horner, R.H., Sugai, G., Bullis, M., et al. (1996). Integrated approaches to preventing antisocial behavior patterns among school-age children and youth. *Journal of Emotional and Behavioral Disorders, 4,* 194–209.

Zins, J.E., Bloodworth, M.R., Weissberg, R.P., & Walberg, H.J. (2004). The scientific base linking social and emotional learning to school success. In J. Zins, M. Wang, & H. Walberg (Eds.), *Building academic success and social-emotional learning: What does the research say?* New York: Teachers College Press.

An Evidence-Based Program

We applaud the current movement toward the use of scientifically based curricula and programs in education and mental health services. SEL programs that are built on good scientific principles of instruction and behavior change and that have demonstrated evidence of effectiveness to support them are a key to making the kind of impact that we believe is necessary to help prevent and remediate the broad range of social, emotional, and mental health problems that plague our society. Several professional organizations have developed standards for determining whether prevention/intervention programs have sufficient evidence behind them to be considered effective from a scientific standpoint. Some of the names that have been used for programs that meet these standards include *empirically validated treatment, empirically supported treatment,* and our own preference, the more generic term, *evidence-based program.*

Since the initial development of the Strong Kids curriculum (including *Strong Start—Pre-K, Strong Start—Grades K–2, Strong Kids—Grades 3–5, Strong Kids—Grades 6–8,* and *Strong Teens—Grades 9–12*), we have made extensive efforts to experimentally test the effectiveness of this program. Several studies have been conducted on the effectiveness of various versions of the Strong Kids program, under a variety of conditions, and more research is in progress. The studies conducted to date (as of 2008) have shown that groups of students who participated in *Strong Kids—Grades 3–5, Strong Kids—Grades 6–8,* and *Strong Teens* have shown significant gains in their knowledge of curriculum concepts of SEL. Some of the studies have shown significant reductions of problem emotional-behavioral symptoms as a result of participating in the programs. In addition, some of the studies have evaluated the social validity of the programs from teacher and student perspectives. These studies, without exception, showed a very high amount of satisfaction and confidence in the programs by both students and teachers.

We encourage interested curriculum users and others to read detailed descriptions of these studies on our web site at http://strongkids.uoregon.edu. As we have already noted, our research efforts with the Strong Kids curriculum are continuing, and we hope to greatly expand the available evidence in support of this program. We will post summaries and reports of research studies on the Strong Kids web site as they become available.

Preparing Your
Lessons and Your Students

Strong Start—Pre-K is designed to be used primarily with children in preschool or about age 3 through age 5. Obviously, there are important differences in the skills and developmental level of children at the two ends of the intended age range. The scripts, examples, and suggested activities we have included in each lesson will work effectively with most children in the intended age range of 3–5 years. We also realize that in some cases the lessons will be more effective for students with very specific needs or developmental issues—such as those who are on the younger end of this age range—if teachers or group leaders modify their delivery of the lessons to tailor them to the specific needs of the children. By simplifying examples and language and reducing some of the time or behavioral demands of different lesson components, *Strong Start—Pre-K* can be used effectively with children at the younger end of the age range. Likewise, the curriculum can be made more relevant for typically developing and high-performing children at the higher end of the age range by using components that require some basic reading skills, increasing the range and complexity of examples and language, and increasing the time and participation demands. As you prepare in advance to teach a *Strong Start—Pre-K* lesson, consider the developmental level of your children, and feel free to make minor adaptations that you believe are appropriate or necessary for your students.

MATERIALS NEEDED

To implement *Strong Start—Pre-K*, you should have access to a copy machine. Many of the lessons provide templates that can be made into laminated cards or overhead transparencies. For your convenience, a CD-ROM included with this manual provides PDF files of the supplements and templates used in *Strong Start—Pre-K*. You may use these PDF files to print the supplements on paper or to project them onto a wall or screen if you have access to a computer projector. Although it is not essential to make laminated cards, we have found that doing so provides the advantage of being able to go over a graphic illustration or chart in front of the class while you introduce the critical concepts that are connected to them. All of the lessons include a *Strong Start* Bulletin to be personalized, duplicated, and sent home to parents to reinforce the lesson goals. The *Strong Start* Bulletins can also be found on the accompanying CD-ROM.

An important part of our lesson development throughout *Strong Start—Pre-K* is the use of a stuffed animal "mascot" for the curriculum. In the lessons, we have given the example of a stuffed bear by the name of Henry. You may follow our suggestion by locating a stuffed bear and naming it Henry, or you may use any type of stuffed animal and name that you think is most appropriate for your children. We have found that children especially enjoy this aspect of the curriculum. Teachers can use the mascot to help in modeling key skills. Furthermore, the mascot becomes not only a symbol for the program but also a reminder to practice *Strong Start* skills and a welcome part of your classroom or group environment.

Some teachers who have assisted us in piloting the initial versions of *Strong Start* found that displaying the stuffed animal in a prominent place in the classroom served as a constant reminder of the program and the skills that were being taught and that their students often asked about the next lesson or previous activities by the prompt of this display. In addition, we recommend that you not only use the mascot when teaching *Strong Start—Pre-K* but also throughout the school year. Picking up the stuffed animal from time to time, weeks or months after completing *Strong Start—Pre-K*, can serve as a keen reminder of what was learned in the program and can help support continued practice and discussion of the critical concepts and skills that were taught.

SUPPLEMENTARY MATERIALS

Each *Strong Start—Pre-K* lesson includes one or more sheets of related or supplementary materials, which are found at the end of the lesson and on the accompanying CD-ROM. These materials are labeled throughout the text with a "reminder" symbol. For the sake of consistency, we refer to these materials as "supplements" and have titled them that way. These supplements include overhead transparency masters and the *Strong Start* Bulletins for parents and family members. As you prepare for each lesson, note the supplements for that lesson and how they should be used. Prior to teaching the lesson, make laminated copies or transparency masters as needed. These supplements are all reproducible for users of the curriculum. Although we have made suggestions regarding how to use the supplementary materials, you should feel free to adapt them to your own needs and situation. For example, you might find it useful to enlarge some of the handouts or transparency masters into posters and to place them on the wall of the classroom to reinforce or visually prompt students as they learn and practice the skills promoted in *Strong Start—Pre-K*.

PROVIDING AN AGENDA

It is recommended that you inform your students before the class begins what the agenda or goals will be for that day's lesson.

STATING EXPECTED BEHAVIORS

Because of the nature of the lessons in *Strong Start—Pre-K*, behavior expectations for students or group members must be very clear. Some of the units revolve around sensitive issues, and every opportunity should be taken to provide instruction and subsequent reinforcement for appropriate behavior. Students should feel free to share their beliefs and feelings on the targeted topics but must not feel pressured into revealing anything that makes them feel uncomfortable. You should state expected behaviors prior to instruction, before modeling examples, and before the practice sections of lessons. In some cases, you may need to teach and reinforce behavioral expectations more frequently than these suggested times.

As a general recommendation for promoting appropriate behavior in school and related settings, we recommend that teachers and group leaders develop and teach a few simple rules for appropriate behavior. Rules should be stated *positively*, meaning that they should tell students what is expected rather than what to avoid. For example, *keep your body safe* and *use nice words* are positively stated rules, whereas *no fighting* is a negatively stated rule that does not tell students what specifically they should do. Rules should be simple and appropriate to the developmental level of the children for whom they are intended. In addition, the list of rules should be kept to a minimum. For preschool-age children, usually, no more than three general rules are needed. You will find that rules are more effective when you teach them to students, then find frequent opportunities to reinforce the rules through reminders, examples, and so forth.

PLANNING FOR SMOOTH TRANSITIONS

Time is one of the most precious commodities in your classroom or center. In a brief curriculum such as *Strong Start—Pre-K*, the element of time is especially critical. To make the best use of your limited time in teaching the curriculum, use your transition time wisely prior to and during the *Strong Start—Pre-K* lessons. We recommend that you have all materials prepared and organized for easy distribution to students. Make sure that equipment is in working order before you start the lessons. You should explicitly state directions prior to and during transitions. If possible, precorrect for any possible behavioral difficulties.

PHYSICAL ARRANGEMENTS

For the lessons in this curriculum, all students must have a clear view of you, the group leader. Forward facing seats or a horseshoe shape are both appropriate. For younger children, seating them in a semi-circle or horseshoe arrangement on the floor for parts of the lessons (e.g., the children's books, the demonstrations) may be appropriate. Always use movement, voice level, and voice intonation to increase the interest of your students, and consequently increase active participation.

ADAPTATIONS FOR UNIQUE NEEDS

In many of the *Strong Start—Pre-K* lessons, you will be encouraged to create scenarios pertaining to a certain topic. To facilitate and encourage student participation, think of scenarios that would best reflect the interests, abilities, and level of understanding of the students in your class or group. You may choose to use current situations relevant to your classroom or school or even global current events to illustrate the concepts. The scenarios provided in the units should be considered examples and can be modified extensively to best fit the unique needs of your students. Making appropriate adaptations for the unique needs of your students will not only make the delivery of lessons go more smoothly but will aid with generalization and maintenance of new skills.

SUGGESTIONS FOR SUCCESS

As you teach the *Strong Start—Pre-K* lessons, you will increase your likelihood of success by observing and following a few additional suggestions for successful implementation of the curriculum:

- Be sure to give the children an *overview* of each lesson's purpose. Explain that a different topic/unit will be taught each week (or as frequently as possible) as students may come to expect a continuation of a certain topic as opposed to a new topic each lesson.

- Our experience has indicated that folders that are specifically designated for students to store their handouts, drawings, notes, and other materials related to *Strong Start—Pre-K* will help them to keep their materials organized and will reduce the amount of time needed by the teacher or group leader to start the weekly lessons. We suggest that you consider having all of your students keep a special *Strong Start folder* for this purpose.

- Ensure that you sufficiently *review the topics* from prior lessons and integrate concepts when at all possible.

- Introduce or reintroduce a *behavior management technique*, such as a token economy, to reinforce prosocial behaviors during the unit. Remind students of school and classroom rules as well as the rules associated with this curriculum.

- This curriculum involves teaching a wide range of skills in a relatively short period of time. In order to use your time most effectively, *directly teach these skills.* Place your priority on instruction, and keep discussion and activity time to a minimum.

- *Reinforce* any *Strong Start—Pre-K* skills that you might observe, both within and outside of the teaching setting. Make sure that parents, teachers, administrators, and other staff are aware of the skills you are instructing, as your students will require frequent feedback in several settings in order for the skills to be durable and generalized.

- Look for opportunities to *use the Applying What We Learned* section found at the end of each lesson. These suggestions have been designed to facilitate the transfer of skills learned through the program across different settings and to help students maintain what they have learned over time. Again, the three areas we have included in Applying What We Learned include prompts for precorrecting errors in learning the expected skills, reminding students of the concepts being learned, and acknowledging students for demonstrating the skills that have been introduced and taught in the program.

- Use and personalize the *Strong Start Bulletins*, which are found at the end of each lesson and on the accompanying CD-ROM. These bulletins, which are in the form of a brief letter, are designed to inform parents and other family members regarding the objectives and activities of each lesson. If parents use the information from these bulletins to reinforce concepts from the lessons and praise their children for engaging in lesson-related skill development, increased generalization of skills across settings may result.

- Use the recommended *children's books*, and add your own titles as appropriate. Each lesson in *Strong Start—Pre-K* includes a 10- to 15-minute period designed to be used to read your students a book that reinforces the key concepts from that lesson. We have developed a short list of books for each lesson, and we encourage you to add and use other titles that you think are appropriate. We have a recommended list of discussion questions in each lesson that can be used with any relevant book.

- Our recommended *time allowance* for each of the lessons is approximately 25–30 minutes. Our experience (and the time breakdowns in the lesson plans) is based on this time length. These time allowances are only guidelines. If your children are very engaged in a particular activity and you are not under time pressure to finish it on schedule, you should feel free to let the activity continue. Likewise, if your children are having a particularly difficult time with one part of a lesson and you have additional time to spare, you should feel free to either continue beyond the time recommendation or to come back to the lesson later in the day. Additional activities are included with most lessons, and it is recommended that these be completed within 2 days of lesson implementation.

- And, of course, *practice your lessons* before implementing them!

ADAPTATIONS FOR CULTURALLY AND LINGUISTICALLY DIVERSE LEARNERS

As our society becomes increasingly diverse, researchers and practitioners have recognized the need to address cultural issues in curriculum development and implementation. Efforts to address cultural issues have ranged from ignoring or dismissing the need for cultural adaptations to arguing the need for culture-specific research and curricula tailored for each cultural subgroup. Between these two extreme positions has emerged a set of criteria and recommendations for making cultural adaptations to existing curricula. The cultural adaptation approach retains the core assumptions and skill domains of the existing curriculum but recommends tailoring the teaching of these concepts to the specific needs of particular groups of interest. Research supports the success of making cultural adaptations to existing social and emotional curricula for specific groups (see Munoz, Penilla, & Urizar, 2002; Yu & Seligman, 2002).

We began the development of the *Strong Kids—Grades 3–5*, *Strong Kids—Grades 6–8*, and *Strong Teens* curricula—the predecessors to *Strong Start*—with the assumption that no single curriculum could meet the learning needs of all students. By focusing on teaching a set of key ideas related to SEL and resiliency, however, we believe that the curricula can successfully meet the needs of a wide range of students when appropriate adaptations are made. Some cultural variables that may require attention in curriculum adaptation processes include language, race/ethnicity, acculturation, socioeconomic status, sexual orientation, religion, gender, disability status, and nationality.

The "Big Ideas" of *Strong Start*

As we have noted, a successful curriculum adaptation process requires particular innovations and modifications to meet the needs of specific individuals and groups, but at the same time, these adaptations must retain the general concepts, or big ideas, on which the curriculum is based. With this notion in mind, we list the most important features of the *Strong Start—Pre-K* curriculum, with the hope that these ideas will be taken into account when making any type of adaptation to the curriculum. With the underlying goal of improving SEL and resiliency in preschool children, these big ideas include the following:

- To help children to understand that social and emotional health, like physical health, requires attention and results from specific actions and situations
- To teach children to identify and understand their own feelings
- To teach children how to identify and understand other people's feelings
- To teach children appropriate ways to express a range of feelings
- To teach children to understand the link between how they think and behave and the way that they feel
- To teach children skills to appropriately monitor and modify their feelings, thoughts, and behaviors
- To help children begin to learn about approaching their challenges in life with a realistic sense of optimism
- To help children to learn behavioral and affective techniques to relax and remain calm in the face of stress or worries
- To teach children problem-solving skills and effective communication skills (e.g., listening, using appropriate vocalization techniques)
- To help children to learn the skills needed to make friends and be a good friend

Specific Strategies for Making Cultural Adaptations

Keeping these big ideas in mind, the *Strong Start—Pre-K* curriculum may be adapted to better fit the needs of diverse children. For this purpose, we propose a few guidelines for making cross-cultural adaptations. These suggestions are based on our experiences in attempting to adapt *Strong Kids—Grades 3–5*, *Strong Kids—Grades 6–8*, and *Strong Teens* with specific cultural groups. They are also based in great measure on the premises of the American Psychological Association's Guidelines for Providers of Psychological Services to Ethnic, Linguistic, and Culturally Diverse Populations (available at http://www.apa.org).

1. Get to know your students.

   - Ask children about their cultural identities, activities, and rituals.

   - Reflect on the dominant cultural variables in your classroom and how these aspects of culture affect the way your students behave and think.

   - Identify common success and failure experiences, problem situations, and challenging life circumstances confronted by your students.

2. Get to know your students' community.

   - Visit the families and, as appropriate, the homes of children in your class or group.

   - Identify a cultural liaison (a parent or community member who identifies as a member of the target cultural group) to help you learn more about your students' culture.

   - Ask the cultural liaison to assist with the cultural adaptation process.

3. Deliver the curriculum in a manner that your students can understand.

   - Modify the language of each lesson so that your students can easily understand the key ideas.

   - Use examples and scenarios that match the lives of your students (e.g., change characters' names, include extended family, include children who use wheelchairs, use problem examples that your students have experienced).

4. Encourage tolerance.

   - Teach students ways to show respect for different cultural groups.

   - Encourage and reinforce children for respecting the examples and comments made by their peers.

   - Establish and enforce a classroom or group rule that teasing and name-calling are not allowed.

5. Become aware of variations within cultures.

   - Do not assume too much about a child's culture or ethnicity.

   - Avoid making overgeneralizations about cultural groups. Not all members of a culture act the same way.

   - Examine your own values, assumptions, and worldviews and how these are the same and different from those of your students.

   - Continually examine the accuracy and fairness of your assumptions about the beliefs and behaviors of different cultural groups.

6. Seek feedback.

- View the adaptation process as an ongoing process.

- Consult with children, your colleagues, and community members about the relevance and accuracy of the adaptation efforts.

- Ask the children how well the curriculum is matching their needs and life experiences.

In sum, adapting *Strong Start—Pre-K* or any other SEL curriculum for use with culturally and linguistically diverse learners may be challenging, but it is essential if the curricula are to have the most meaningful impact on the learners. The suggestions we have offered in this section may be useful as a guide to making the flexible *Strong Start—Pre-K* program appropriate for children and youth from a variety of cultural backgrounds.

REFERENCES

Munoz, R.F., Penilla, C., & Urizar, G. (2002, May 8). Expanding depression prevention research with children of diverse cultures. *Prevention and Treatment, 5.* Retrieved November 19, 2005, from http://www.journals.apa.org/prevention/volume5/pre0050013c.html

Yu, D.L., & Seligman, M.E.P. (2002). Preventing depressive symptoms in Chinese children. *Prevention and Treatment, 5.* Retrieved November 19, 2005, from http://www.journals.apa.org/prevention/volume5/pre0050009a.html

Overview of the Lessons

*S*trong Start—Pre-K consists of 10 carefully sequenced lessons, designed to enhance children's cognitive, affective, and social functioning within a relatively brief period of time. Each of these lessons is overviewed in this section. You should read these descriptions carefully prior to preparing your first lesson so that you will understand the lesson sequencing and the "big ideas" behind *Strong Start—Pre-K.*

LESSON 1: THE FEELINGS EXERCISE GROUP

In the first lesson, The Feelings Exercise Group, students are introduced to the *Strong Start—Pre-K* curriculum, and the purpose, goals, and practices of the program are overviewed. A general overview of the big ideas of the curriculum and its individual lessons is provided so that students will understand what they can expect over the course of the instruction as well as behavioral expectations for their participation. Important terms are introduced, as is Henry, a stuffed animal that serves as the mascot for the curriculum and is used to help introduce key concepts. Students are made aware of the importance of this curriculum so that they are able to understand why appropriate behaviors such as showing good listening, keeping a calm body, and being a friend, as well as confidentiality of shared information, are integral parts of the experience.

LESSONS 2 AND 3: UNDERSTANDING YOUR FEELINGS

The second and third lessons, Understanding Your Feelings 1 and 2, are intended to improve the emotional vocabulary, awareness, and resiliency skills of students. Understanding and recognizing one's emotions is an important skill for everyone during all stages of life because people experience emotions at school, home, work, and play. Being able to recognize their emotions and react in an appropriate way, even when the emotion is not a good feeling, will allow your students to create and sustain positive relationships in school and throughout their lives.

In Understanding Your Feelings 1, students learn to identify different types of basic emotions and distinguish them as resulting in "good" or "not good" feelings. Students learn to recognize which situations might cause them to feel a certain way. The goal of this lesson is to apply the skills learned to different situations at different times and in different settings.

In Understanding Your Feelings 2, the feelings-identification skills are extended to include how one might express different feelings—both positive and negative—in an appropriate manner. Students learn that, although it is okay to have any feeling, there are appropriate and inappropriate ways of showing or expressing feelings. Given a way of expressing a feeling, students identify the way as "okay" or "not okay." Students then have the opportunity to apply their new skills in fun application exercises, making it more likely that they will be able to generalize the new skills to other situations.

LESSON 4: WHEN YOU'RE ANGRY

The fourth lesson, When You're Angry, teaches students that all people experience anger in their lives; however, many young children are not able to appropriately understand and deal effectively with their anger. Misunderstanding anger, and an inability to appropriately manage it, can often manifest itself in inappropriate behaviors such as arguments and fights, excessive sadness, and frustration. This lesson teaches students to understand the physical signs or manifestations of anger in their bodies, identify common situations that might lead people to feel angry, and determine if responses to anger are done in "Ways that Help" or "Ways that Hurt." Students also learn synonyms for *anger*. Through activities and stories, a particular emphasis is placed on developing and practicing responses to anger that are Ways that Help.

LESSON 5: WHEN YOU'RE HAPPY

The fifth lesson, When You're Happy, teaches students how to understand and express the positive emotion of happiness. Although virtually all preschool and kindergarten students can identify the feeling of happiness, most have not yet learned the connection between this emotion and their thought processes and behaviors. This lesson focuses on identifying common physical or bodily sensations associated with feeling happy, actions and situations that are more likely to lead to this positive feeling, and developing synonyms for the word *happy*. In addition, students are taught a simple technique—Happy Talk—that can help them cope with adverse situations in a positive way while being less likely to succumb to negative feelings such as sadness or anger.

LESSON 6: WHEN YOU'RE WORRIED

Learning appropriate techniques to manage stress, anxiety, and common worries is an important strategy to promote emotional resilience and prevent physical and emotional problems. In Lesson 6, When You're Worried, students are taught to apply specific behavioral, affective, and cognitive skills to situations that might cause them worry and anxiety. The same techniques that were taught for other specific feelings—understanding physical sensations, developing synonyms, and listing common situations in which the feeling might occur—are applied specifically to the emotion of worry or anxiety. Students again practice using Happy Talk, and they are taught a new skill—the Stop, Count, In, Out strategy—that they can apply specifically to help cope with worries, fears, stress, and anxiety.

LESSON 7: UNDERSTANDING OTHER PEOPLE'S FEELINGS

The seventh lesson, Understanding Other People's Feelings, is a very basic form of empathy training, or teaching young children to discern and understand the feelings that other people experience. Many, if not most, kindergarten and primary grade students have not yet adequately learned to take the perspective of other people, so this lesson is an important step in beginning to acquire this critical people skill. Students are taught to identify common physical cues or clues to help understand how another person might be feeling. Through stories and fun activities, students are given practice in this skill to help increase the chance that they will maintain it and generalize it to other settings.

LESSON 8: BEING A GOOD FRIEND

The eighth lesson, Being a Good Friend, is a very basic social skills and interpersonal skills training module for young children. In this lesson, students are taught some of the most basic interpersonal communication skills and given opportunities to practice them in realistic situations. Skills such as using a nice voice, being a good listener, making appropriate eye contact, and using appropriate body language are emphasized. A particular focus is placed on skills that will help students make friends more easily and be good friends.

LESSON 9: SOLVING PEOPLE PROBLEMS

The ninth lesson, Solving People Problems, is designed to promote awareness of useful strategies for resolving conflict between and among peers. Interpersonal conflicts can begin early in life and, if they become a continual pattern, may provide a fertile breeding ground for depression, anxiety, and negative thinking. Thus, learning appropriate and effective ways to resolve these conflicts may be a strong preventive factor for deterring emotional as well as social problems. In this lesson, students define and describe situations in which conflicts with peers might commonly occur. Through a review of the previously taught skills for coping with anger and using Happy Talk, students are taught to apply these strategies to help fix peer problems. This lesson includes practice situations where students can learn to identify common problems that may arise with peers, and they can practice thinking about how to fix these problems and feel better.

LESSON 10: FINISHING UP!

The title of the final *Strong Start—Pre-K* lesson, Finishing UP!, has a double meaning. It implies that this lesson is the final one in the curriculum, but it also shows how we are striving to end on a positive or upbeat note, celebrating the accomplishments that have been made through involvement with the *Strong Start—Pre-K* curriculum. This lesson provides the opportunity for students to review key points and terms from the lessons presented throughout the previous several weeks. The specific *Strong Start—Pre-K* skills that students were taught in previous lessons—identifying okay and not okay feelings; defining Ways that Help and Ways that Hurt; and using Happy Talk and the Stop, Count, In, Out strategy—are all reviewed one last time to ensure competency. Henry, the stuffed animal mascot, figures prominently in this lesson and will be available to students in the future as a tangible prompt regarding the things they learned and practiced in the *Strong Start—Pre-K* curriculum.

BOOSTER LESSONS

Appendices A and B include optional Booster Lessons for use with *Strong Start—Pre-K*. These Booster Lessons cover six and three *Strong Start—Pre-K* lessons, respectively. They are designed to be taught several weeks or months following the conclusion of the 10 *Strong Start—Pre-K* lessons, in order to help reteach and reinforce the main concepts from *Strong Start—Pre-K*. Although the Booster Lessons are optional components, we highly recommend them and urge teachers and group leaders to consider using them to make the curriculum optimally effective. We suggest that Booster Lesson 1 be taught at least 1 month after the conclusion of the 10 *Strong Start—Pre-K* lessons, and we also recommend using the Booster Lessons as two separate sessions, instead of combining them into one lesson. In addition to reteaching and reinforcing the critical components of *Strong Start—Pre-K*, your students will find the Booster Lessons to be fun. We have developed a game, Strong Start Feelings Bingo, for use specifically in the Booster Lessons, to help reteach the six basic emotions that are taught in *Strong Start—Pre-K*.

APPLYING WHAT WE LEARNED

As a teacher or group leader, you want your efforts in teaching *Strong Start—Pre-K* to result in the students continuing to use their new adaptive social-emotional skills over time and in other settings. In developing *Strong Start—Pre-K*, we specifically planned and programmed the curricula for optimal application by children across settings and over time. In technical terms, this sort of application is referred to as *maintenance and generalization*. Specifically, we have included suggestions and activities within each of the 10 *Strong Start—Pre-K* lessons that are aimed at promoting the application or generalization of new skills learned across settings other than the intervention setting (e.g., home, community, other school settings) and the maintenance of these skills over time.

At the end of each of the 10 lessons is a section titled Applying What We Learned. This brief section includes suggested activities and methods in the following three areas, which are based on literature on effective instructional approaches for teaching social-behavioral skills authored by Sugai and colleagues (e.g., Langland, Lewis-Palmer, & Sugai, 1998; Sugai, Bullis, & Cumblad, 1997):

- *Anticipate*—activities designed to help the instructor/group leader anticipate errors and difficulties that students may have in learning new skills, to maximize the efficacy in teaching new skills that are sequenced instructionally to previously taught skills

- *Remind*—suggestions for providing verbal or visual prompts to students that will help remind them of steps, sequences, skills, and actions that are needed to engage effectively in new skills as they are taught

- *Acknowledge*—prompts to provide acknowledgment or praise as students successfully approximate and perform the new skills they are taught in *Strong Start—Pre-K*

In addition to the suggestions in the Applying What We Learned sections, each lesson has, embedded within it, tips for instructors as they develop and model examples of new skills and help the students see the need for these skills. These suggestions are aimed at making the lessons relevant to students, thus increasing the potential effectiveness of each lesson. Appropriate activities are provided for each of the 10 lessons that are further designed to reinforce learning from the direct instructional part of the lessons. Each lesson also has a *Strong Start* Bulletin included as a supplement. These bulletins are important communication links to the home setting to help generalize new skills your students learn.

FINAL COMMENTS

Good luck as you prepare to use *Strong Start—Pre-K*. We have field-tested this curriculum with teachers and mental health professionals in the United States and elsewhere and have made many improvements to it based on their feedback from experience using it with a large number of children and in a large variety of settings. Our efforts to create an effective, user-friendly, and practical mental health promotion program, coupled with the real-world experience and feedback we gained during 5 years of initial research and development, have convinced us that the Strong Kids curriculum has much to offer and can be a valuable tool for supporting SEL, promoting resilience, and teaching coping skills.

REFERENCES

Langland, S., Lewis-Palmer, T., & Sugai, G. (1998). Teaching respect in the classroom: An instructional approach. *Journal of Behavioral Education, 8,* 245–262.

Sugai, G., Bullis, M., & Cumblad, C. (1997). Provide ongoing skill development and support. *Journal of Emotional and Behavioral Disorders, 5,* 55–64.

The *Strong Start— Pre-K* Curriculum

LESSON 1

The Feelings Exercise Group

TEACHER NOTES

⭐ Purpose

- To introduce students to the *Strong Start—Pre-K* curriculum

⭐ Objectives

- Students will identify the purpose of the *Strong Start— Pre-K* curriculum.
- Students will learn expected behaviors for participation in the program.
- Students will demonstrate a developmentally appropriate understanding of the concept of confidentiality.

MATERIALS NEEDED

- ❑ Henry (stuffed animal mascot)
- ❑ Book from the literature list (or one of your choice)
- ❑ Supplement 1.1 (laminated card)
- ❑ *Strong Start* Bulletin

Introduction

3 minutes

Communicate the lesson's purpose and objectives clearly. Explain to your students that they will be starting a new curriculum, *Strong Start*. Tell them how often it will be taught, and give examples of some of the topics that will be covered. Make it clear that the skills learned during this unit are skills that are important to their social and emotional health during all phases of life.

Throughout the lessons, we use a small stuffed bear named Henry as a class mascot. You may select a different stuffed animal or name if you wish. Introduce the children to Henry.

Sample Script

Today, we are going to begin a special class called Strong Start. In this class, we will be learning with a new friend. His name is Henry! In this class, Henry will help us understand our feelings and other people's feelings. He will also help us learn about being a good friend. We will be with Henry [once per week] for [one class period]. Every time we meet, we will do special exercises, except we won't be running around outside or lifting big, heavy weights. We will be working on growing strong on the inside, so we will call our group the Feelings Exercise Group. Everyone needs to be healthy—on the outside and on the inside. This class will help you to be healthy on the inside for your whole life.

Read a Book from the Literature List

10 minutes

Read a book from the following list of examples or choose your own book to share with students.

- *Feelings* by Aliki
- *The Way I Feel* by Janan Cain
- *Feelings* by Joanne Brisson Murphy
- *The Feelings Book* by Todd Parr
- *My Many Colored Days* by Dr. Seuss

Be sure to point out all of the actions or ways in which the characters behave when they are acting on their feelings. Use the following questions to guide your discussion:

- What was one of the feelings the character had?
- Do you think it was a **good** or **not good** feeling?
- What did the character do when he or she was feeling that way?

Defining Behavior Expectations

5 minutes

Explain to your students that they are now part of a special group with some special rules. It is helpful to present the rules one at a time and have your students help you to determine and demonstrate examples and nonexamples of each rule. The three rules for the group are as follows:

1. Be a good listener.

2. Keep a calm body.

3. Be a friend.

Sample Script

You are now part of a special group with some special rules. The first rule is "Be a good listener." What does a good listener do? (Expect answers like eyes on the person who is talking and lips zipped.) The next rule is "Keep a calm body." What does a calm body look like? (Expect answers like hands to ourselves and sitting on our bottoms.) Why do you think it is important to have a calm body when we are in the Feelings Exercise Group? The last rule is "Be a good friend." What does it mean to be a good friend? How can you be a good friend? (Expect answers like someone who listens to you and someone who is nice to you.)

Discuss the Concept of Confidentiality

Help your students understand the following ideas:

• They may be asked to share personal information during lessons.

• They have the right to pass on sharing personal stories.

• They may speak to you individually if they feel uncomfortable sharing in a large group.

Have students demonstrate that they understand these concepts.

Sample Script

During this special class, you might be asked to share stories about times when you have been very happy, mad, or sad or have had other very strong feelings, such as being scared. If you want to share a story, you can raise your hand to let me know. If you start to feel like you don't want to share a story anymore, you can stop at any time. If you don't want to tell everyone your story, but you would still like to share it with me, you can talk to me after class.

When someone else is sharing a story, we will follow our special group rules—we will be good listeners, we will keep calm bodies, and we will be good friends.

Introduction to the Topics Covered in the Curriculum

Introduce the topics, and provide a brief explanation for each of the lessons using Supplement 1.1 as a laminated card.

Sample Script

When we meet for Strong Start lessons, we will be learning lots of new things. We will learn about feeling angry, feeling happy, and feeling worried or scared. We will learn about other people's feelings, and we will learn about being a friend. We will also learn about solving problems. Finally, we will learn how to relax and feel calm.

Closure

1 minute

Gather your students together, and review the lesson's objectives.

Sample Script

Today, we talked about our new special class called Strong Start, which is a Feelings Exercise Group. We also talked about the rules of our group, which are 1) be a good listener, 2) keep a calm body, and 3) be a friend. This class will help us learn how to be healthy on the inside for the rest of our lives, and Henry is going to help us. I am excited to start this special class with you!

 **About Strong Start**

We will learn about our feelings.

feeling *angry*   feeling *happy*   feeling *worried*

We will learn about other people's feelings.

We will learn about being a friend.

We will learn about solving problems.

And we will learn how to relax and feel calm.

Strong Start—Pre-K: A Social and Emotional Learning Curriculum

 **Strong Start Bulletin**

Dear Family,

Today, your child participated in the first lesson of **Strong Start**, a curriculum designed to boost the social and emotional development of young children. This curriculum includes 10 lessons that help children in recognizing and managing emotions, engaging in problem solving, and being a good friend. Your child was introduced to **Henry,** a stuffed bear who will serve as an important figure in the classroom community and in all lessons included in this curriculum. Today's lesson, entitled **The Feelings Exercise Group,** focused on helping children realize that it is just as important to be emotionally strong as it is to be physically strong. Below are examples of the vocabulary and pictures presented during today's lesson.

Strong Start's Objectives

To learn about our feelings

To learn about other people's feelings

To learn about being a friend

To learn about solving problems

And to learn how to relax and feel calm

Over the next several weeks, you will be receiving bulletins that detail the content of all of the Strong Start lessons. To help your child use the skills he or she learns, be sure to read the letters and try out the suggested strategies at home.

Thank you in advance for supporting your child as he or she learns about the important topics covered in Strong Start. If you notice your child using skills he or she has learned at school, be sure to applaud your child's efforts!

Strong Start—Pre-K: A Social and Emotional Learning Curriculum
by Kenneth W. Merrell, Sara A. Whitcomb, and Danielle M. Parisi © 2009 University of Oregon. All rights reserved.

LESSON 2

Understanding Your Feelings 1

★ Purpose

- To teach students to name basic feelings

★ Objectives

- Students will name six feelings.
- Students will identify feelings that make them feel *good* or *not good* on the inside.

MATERIALS NEEDED

- ❑ Henry (stuffed animal mascot)
- ❑ Blank overhead transparency or chart paper
- ❑ Book from the literature list (or one of your choice)
- ❑ Supplements 2.1–2.6 (feelings pictures on laminated cards)
- ❑ Supplement 2.7 (cutout feelings pictures, six feelings per student)
- ❑ Paper plates
- ❑ Glue or glue sticks
- ❑ Contruction paper arrows (one per student)
- ❑ Brad fasteners (one per student)
- ❑ *Strong Start* Bulletin

Review

To activate prior knowledge, review and discuss previous topics and main ideas. Obtain 1–2 adequate ideas. Make sure to provide feedback.

Sample Script

During our last meeting, we introduced you to the Feelings Exercise Group. Raise your hand if you can tell me an important idea we learned during that lesson.

Introduction

Communicate the lesson's purpose and objectives clearly.

Sample Script

*Today, Henry has come back to help us learn how to name our feelings. We will talk about all different kinds of feelings and how they make us feel **good** or **not good** on the inside.*

Read a Book from the Literature List

Read a book from the following list of examples or choose your own book to share with students.

- *My First Day at Nursery School* by Becky Edwards
- *Feelings* by Aliki
- *Everybody Has Feelings or Todos Tenemos Sentimientos* by Charles E. Avery
- *How Are You Peeling? Foods with Moods* by Saxton Freymann and Joost Elffers
- *On Monday When It Rained* by Cherryl Kachenmeister
- *Feelings* by Joanne Brisson Murphy
- *The Feelings Book* by Todd Parr
- *Lots of Feelings* by Shelley Rotner

Be sure to point out all of the actions or ways in which the characters behave when they are acting on their feelings. Use the following questions to guide your discussion:

- What was one of the feelings the character had?
- Do you think it was a **good** or **not good** feeling?
- What did the character do when he or she was feeling that way?

Feelings Identification

Explain to students that you will be discussing feelings and labeling them as those that make us feel **good** or **not good** on the inside.

Sample Script

Let's talk about naming our feelings. No matter where we are, we always have feelings—at school, at home, and at play..

Use Supplements 2.1–2.6 to guide your discussion about feelings.

1. Generate a list of feelings.

    *   State a basic emotion, such as happy or sad, and explain that this is a feeling. Show the picture that goes with that feeling and help children understand the facial features that help to tell what feeling it is (e.g., a happy face shows a smile).

    *   Give a second example, using a more complex emotion such as angry or surprised. Show a relevant picture.

    *   Repeat this process until you have shown all six feelings pictures.

2. Identify feelings that may make us feel **good** or **not good.**

    *   Model this skill using all of the feelings you and the students named in Step 1.

    ### Sample Script

    *Happy is a **good** feeling. When I feel happy, I feel good, and I like to smile. Sad is a **not good** feeling. When I feel sad, I feel bad, and I may even cry.*

    *   Go back to the start of your list, and have the students stand up for feelings that make people feel **good** on the inside and sit down for feelings that make people feel **not good** on the inside.

    ### Sample Script

    *Another way you could show that feelings are **good** or **not good** is to stand up or sit down. When I show a picture and say the feeling that goes with it, I want you to stand up if it makes you feel **good** and sit down if it makes you feel **not good**. Remember, not all of you will feel the same way about all feelings. For example, when I feel surprised, I feel **good,** but Henry does not like surprised feelings. They make him feel **not good** on the inside.*

If You're Happy and You Know It

Encourage students to stand up and follow your lead in singing *If You're Happy and You Know It*. Use the following script as a guide, and add any additional feelings as you see fit. Display Supplements 2.1–2.6 if desired.

Sample Script

If you're happy and you know it, clap your hands.
If you're sad and you know it, say, "Boo hoo."
If you're afraid and you know it, take a breath.
If you're angry and you know it, use your words.
If you're surprised and you know it, say, "Wowee."
If you're disgusted and you know it, say, "Yucky."

1 minute Closure

Gather your students together, and review the lesson objectives.

Sample Script

*Today, we learned how to name our feelings. We learned how to name different kinds of feelings. We talked about how feelings make us feel **good** or **not good** on the inside, and we talked about times when we have different feelings. Everyone has feelings at school, at home, and at play. Being able to name our feelings is important because if we know how to name our feelings and can talk about them, it will help us to know what to do even if the feeling makes us feel **not good** on the inside.*

15 minutes Additional Activity: How Do You Feel?

Complete this activity within 2 days of lesson implementation.

• Use this time to brainstorm examples of how people might feel at different times. Model examples of times when you felt happy or sad.

Sample Script

We all have feelings every day. Some days we might feel happy, and on other days we might have different feelings. For example, today Henry is feeling happy because he is here with all of you. Yesterday, he felt afraid because he watched a scary movie on TV.

• Encourage children to participate in making a feelings wheel so that they can point an arrow to how they feel. Give each child a paper plate that has been divided into six pie pieces with a marker. Give children cutout pictures of each of the six basic feelings (Supplement 2.7). Have children glue one feeling to each section of their plates, and then help children fasten a construction paper arrow to the center of their plates.

• At the conclusion, show children how they can use their feelings wheels to share how they are feeling on that day. If appropriate and students are willing, invite two or three students to share how they are feeling.

Applying What We Learned

Anticipate

Tell your students to try to name the feelings they experience throughout the day. Once they identify or label the feelings they are experiencing, encourage them to investigate whether the feelings make them feel **good** or **not good** on the inside. This exercise might be particularly helpful on days that will likely include more intense emotions (e.g., field trips).

Remind

If you notice students having difficulty expressing themselves in words (e.g., getting frustrated and showing it by rolling their eyes, feeling tired or upset and expressing it by putting their heads on the table), remind them to tell you what they are feeling using the words, feelings labels, or feelings wheels that were part of the lesson. Initially, it may be helpful to model use of such vocabulary (e.g., "It looks like you are feeling happy today. I can see that you have a big smile. Do you feel **good** on the inside?").

Acknowledge

Praise your students (or give them a small reward if you have a behavior management system in your classroom) if you notice them expressing a feeling or expressing that their feelings make them feel **good** or **not good** on the inside (e.g., "Sally called me a name, and it made me feel **not good** on the inside," or "My mom bought me a new toy, and it made me feel **good** on the inside.").

Basic Feelings

Happy

Basic Feelings

Sad

Strong Start—Pre-K: A Social and Emotional Learning Curriculum

41

 **Basic Feelings**

Afraid

Strong Start—Pre-K: A Social and Emotional Learning Curriculum
by Kenneth W. Merrell, Sara A. Whitcomb, and Danielle M. Parisi © 2009 University of Oregon. All rights reserved.

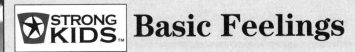 **Basic Feelings**

Angry

Strong Start—Pre-K: A Social and Emotional Learning Curriculum
by Kenneth W. Merrell, Sara A. Whitcomb, and Danielle M. Parisi © 2009 University of Oregon. All rights reserved.

STRONG KIDS™ Basic Feelings

Surprised

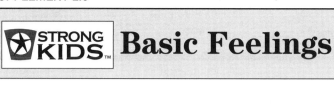 **Basic Feelings**

Disgusted

Strong Start—Pre-K: A Social and Emotional Learning Curriculum
by Kenneth W. Merrell, Sara A. Whitcomb, and Danielle M. Parisi © 2009 University of Oregon. All rights reserved.

 **Basic Feelings Cards**

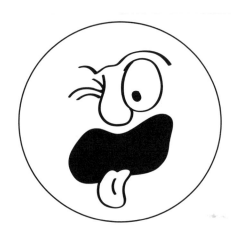

Strong Start—Pre-K: A Social and Emotional Learning Curriculum
by Kenneth W. Merrell, Sara A. Whitcomb, and Danielle M. Parisi © 2009 University of Oregon. All rights reserved.

STRONG START
LESSON 2

 # Strong Start Bulletin

Dear Family,

This week, our **Strong Start** lesson focused on identifying and understanding the **six basic feelings** reflected below. We reviewed the names of feelings and discussed that some make us feel **good** on the inside while others make us feel **not good.** We talked about how we might have different feelings on different days and we also made a feelings wheel to show how we are feeling. Throughout the lesson, Henry helped us understand that it is natural for everyone to experience all feelings.

Basic Emotions

| Happy | Sad | Afraid | Angry | Surprised | Disgusted |

To better understand our feelings, we sang:
If you're happy and you know it, clap your hands.
If you're sad and you know it, say, "Boo hoo."
If you're afraid and you know it, take a breath.
If you're angry and you know it, use your words.
If you're surprised and you know it, say, "Wowee."
If you're disgusted and you know it, say, "Yucky."

At home encourage your child to
- Stop and name the feeling he or she is experiencing.
- Determine whether or not it is a **good** or **not good** feeling.

Thanks for supporting your child as he or she learns about identifying feelings. If you notice your child naming his or her feelings or expressing feelings that make him or her feel **good** or **not good** on the inside, be sure to acknowledge your child's efforts!

LESSON 3

Understanding Your Feelings 2

TEACHER NOTES

⭐ **Purpose**

- To review the six basic feelings
- To teach students appropriate ways of expressing feelings

⭐ **Objectives**

- Students will become fluent in identifying basic feelings.
- Students will be able to distinguish between *okay* and *not okay* ways of expressing feelings.

MATERIALS NEEDED

- ❏ Henry (stuffed animal mascot)
- ❏ Blank overhead transparency or chart paper
- ❏ Book from the literature list (or one of your choice)
- ❏ Supplement 3.1–3.6 (feelings pictures on laminated cards)
- ❏ *Strong Start* Bulletin

Review

2 minutes

To activate prior knowledge, review and discuss previous topics and main ideas. Prompt students to remember the six basic feelings: happy, sad, angry, afraid, surprised, and disgusted. Make sure to provide feedback.

Sample Script

During our last meeting, we learned to name our feelings. Raise your hand if you can remember a feeling that we learned about in our last class.

Introduction

1 minute

Communicate the lesson's purpose and objectives clearly.

Sample Script

Today, we are going to learn more about feelings. I have brought Henry to help us as we do this.

Read a Book from the Literature List

10 minutes

Read a book from the following list of examples or choose your own book to share with students.

- *The Chocolate-Covered-Cookie Tantrum* by Deborah Blumenthal
- *Today I Feel Silly & Other Moods That Make My Day* by Jamie Lee Curtis
- *The Grumpy Morning* by Pamela Duncan Edwards
- *Chrysanthemum* by Kevin Henkes
- *Julius: The Baby of the World* by Kevin Henkes
- *Bye, Bye!* by Nancy Kaufmann
- *The Kissing Hand* by Audrey Penn
- *Sometimes I Like to Cry* by Elizabeth and Henry Stanton

Be sure to point out all of the actions or ways in which the characters behave when they are acting on their feelings. Use the following questions to guide your discussion:

- What was one of the feelings the character had?
- Do you think it was a **good** or **not good** feeling?
- What did the character do when he or she was feeling that way?
- Was it an **okay** or **not okay** way of showing the feeling?

Understanding Basic Emotions

- Revisit *If You're Happy and You Know It.*

- Present pictures of each of the six basic feelings using Supplements 3.1–3.6. Have students give examples of when they may experience these feelings.

Sample Script

*This is a picture of disgust. Disgust is **not a good** feeling. Raise your hand if you can think of a time when you might feel disgust.*

Ways of Showing Feelings

Convey the following main ideas to your students:

- Everyone has feelings, and it is okay to have any feeling.

- We have different feelings at different times.

- It is important to talk about what we are feeling on the inside.

- There are **okay** and **not okay** ways to show feelings.

Sample Script

*Everyone has feelings, and it is **okay** to have any feeling. We have different feelings at different times. When Henry is playing outside, he feels happy, and when it is cold and rainy and he has to stay inside, he feels sad. There are different ways to show our feelings. When Henry eats broccoli, he has a feeling of disgust, which is a yucky feeling. He chews it up and spits it out on the table. This is **not an okay** way of showing disgust because Henry wasn't showing good manners. Instead, when Henry's mom makes broccoli for dinner, Henry can say, "No, thank you." This is an **okay** way of showing disgust because Henry is showing good manners*

Okay and Not Okay Examples of Showing Other Feelings

The following additional examples may reflect similar situations that the children share. Use them to guide your thinking as you plan for this lesson. It might be helpful to use Henry as a puppet and have him act out **okay** and **not okay** ways to show feelings.

Have students stand up if the example suggests an **okay** way of showing feelings and stay seated if the example is **not an okay** way of showing feelings.

Feeling	Example	Okay	Not okay
Sad	Henry's dog runs away.	Henry tells you how he is feeling.	Henry screams and demands a new pet.
Angry	A friend borrowed Henry's toy car without asking.	Henry takes a deep breath and uses nice words to tell his friend how he is feeling.	Henry pulls the car out of his friend's hand.
Surprised	Henry sees his preschool teacher at the grocery store.	Henry gives his teacher a little wave.	Henry hides behind the counter and hopes she will not see him.
Afraid	Henry has to go to the doctor.	Henry tells his parents how he is feeling.	Henry keeps his feelings a secret and gets a tummy ache.

2 minutes

Closure

Gather your students together, and review the lesson objectives.

Sample Script

*We all have feelings. Today, we learned that there are **okay** and **not okay** ways of showing feelings. It is all right to have any feeling, but it is important that we show our feelings in **okay** ways.*

Applying What We Learned

Anticipate

Tell your students to remember to practice naming their feelings and using **okay** ways to show their feelings. It might be helpful to prompt them prior to potentially emotional times of the day, such as at recess, choice time, or when making the transition between activities.

Remind

Similar to the last lesson, if you notice students having difficulty expressing their feelings (e.g., saying, "He is not sharing. I hate him!"), remind them that these are **not okay** ways to express their feelings, and ask them to try it again in an **okay** way. Initially, you might have to model an **okay** way of expressing the particular feeling (e.g., "Watch me and listen. When you don't share, it makes me feel angry.").

Acknowledge

Praise your students for displaying **okay** ways of expressing their feelings. Some examples of **okay** ways could include students using "I feel" statements, talking (not yelling) about their issues with one another, or asking for help if they are getting frustrated.

 **Basic Feelings**

Happy

Strong Start—Pre-K: A Social and Emotional Learning Curriculum
by Kenneth W. Merrell, Sara A. Whitcomb, and Danielle M. Parisi © 2009 University of Oregon. All rights reserved.

★STRONG KIDS™ **Basic Feelings**

Sad

Strong Start—Pre-K: A Social and Emotional Learning Curriculum
by Kenneth W. Merrell, Sara A. Whitcomb, and Danielle M. Parisi © 2009 University of Oregon. All rights reserved.   55

Basic Feelings

Afraid

Basic Feelings

Angry

Strong Start—Pre-K: A Social and Emotional Learning Curriculum
by Kenneth W. Merrell, Sara A. Whitcomb, and Danielle M. Parisi © 2009 University of Oregon. All rights reserved.

STRONG KIDS™ Basic Feelings

Surprised

Strong Start—Pre-K: A Social and Emotional Learning Curriculum
by Kenneth W. Merrell, Sara A. Whitcomb, and Danielle M. Parisi © 2009 University of Oregon. All rights reserved.

STRONG KIDS™ **Basic Feelings**

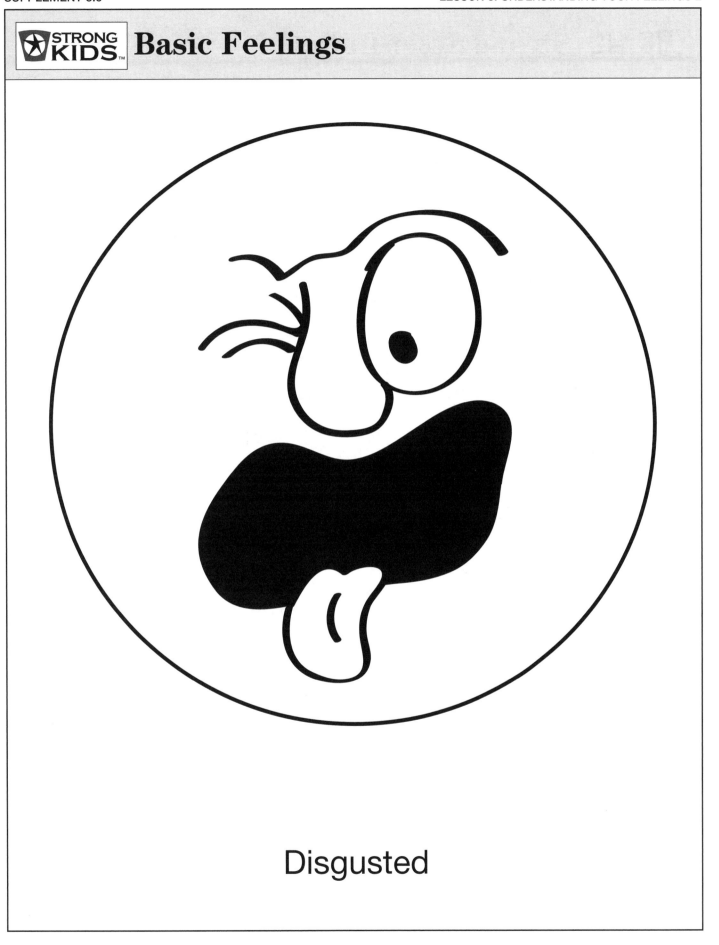

Disgusted

Strong Start—Pre-K: A Social and Emotional Learning Curriculum
by Kenneth W. Merrell, Sara A. Whitcomb, and Danielle M. Parisi © 2009 University of Oregon. All rights reserved.   59

 **Strong Start Bulletin**

Dear Family,

This week, our **Strong Start** lesson extended ideas presented during last week's lesson. We reviewed the names of feelings: **happy, sad, angry, afraid, disgusted,** and **surprised.** We also reviewed those feelings that make us feel **good** or **not good.** Throughout the lesson, Henry helped us understand that it is natural for everyone to experience all feelings. He also helped us to know **okay** and **not okay** ways to act on our feelings. We defined situations that make us experience certain feelings and examples of **okay** and **not okay** ways for handling the situations. Some examples that we discussed are listed in the table.

Feeling	Example	Okay	Not okay
Sad	Your dog runs away.	Telling a parent how you are feeling	Screaming and demanding a new pet
Angry	A friend borrows your toy car without asking.	Taking a deep breath and using nice words to tell your friend how you are feeling	Pulling the car out of your friend's hand

To better understand handling feelings, we read

_____ .

Following are great examples of relevant stories that you may want to read at home:
- *Chrysanthemum* by Kevin Henkes
- *The Chocolate-Covered-Cookie Tantrum* by Deborah Blumenthal
- *Today I Feel Silly & Other Moods That Make My Day* by Jamie Lee Curtis

At home, remind your child to
- Stop and identify the feeling he or she is experiencing.
- Determine whether or not it is a **good** or **not good** feeling.
- Choose an **okay** way to act on that feeling.

Thanks for helping your child to apply what he or she has learned about identifying feelings. Be sure to congratulate your child each time he or she chooses an **okay** way to handle a difficult situation.

Strong Start—Pre-K: A Social and Emotional Learning Curriculum

LESSON 4

When You're Angry

_____

_____

_____

_____

_____

_____

_____

_____

_____

_____

_____

_____

_____

_____

_____

_____

_____

_____

_____

_____

⭐ Purpose

- To teach students how to manage anger and helpful ways of handling anger

⭐ Objectives

- Students will accurately describe how their bodies feel when they are angry.

- Students will accurately list synonyms for the word _anger._

- Students will identify situations that might make people angry.

- Students will understand _Ways that Help_ and _Ways that Hurt_ in handling their anger.

MATERIALS NEEDED

- ❑ Henry (stuffed animal mascot)
- ❑ Blank overhead transparency or chart paper
- ❑ Book from the literature list (or one of your choice)
- ❑ Supplement 4.1 (laminated card)
- ❑ Supplement 4.2 (laminated card)
- ❑ Supplement 4.3 (laminated card)
- ❑ Supplements 4.4–4.7 (Stop, Count, In, Out pictures on laminated cards)
- ❑ Supplement 4.8 (stop sign in-class handout)
- ❑ Red crayons
- ❑ Craft sticks and glue or glue sticks
- ❑ _Strong Start_ Bulletin

2 minutes Review

To activate prior knowledge, review and discuss previous topics and main ideas. Make sure to provide feedback.

Sample Script

*During our last meeting, we discussed how to understand our feelings and **okay** ways for showing them. Raise your hand if you can tell me an **okay** way of showing one of the feelings. How about a **not okay** way? We also learned about **good** and **not good** feelings. Raise your hand if you can remember a **good** feeling. How about a **not good** feeling?*

1 minute Introduction

Communicate the lesson's purpose and objectives clearly.

Sample Script

Today, we will talk about a feeling called anger. Anger is a normal feeling, and everybody feels angry sometimes. We will learn what anger looks like and when it might happen. We will also learn ways to deal with our anger so that we don't hurt ourselves or others.

10 minutes Read a Book from the Literature List

Read a book from the following list of examples or choose your own to share with students.

- *The Cranky Day and Other Thomas the Tank Engine Stories* by W. Awdry
- *When Sophie Gets Angry—Really, Really Angry* by Molly Bang
- *The Chocolate-Covered-Cookie Tantrum* by Deborah Blumenthal
- *Feeling Angry* by Althea Braithwaite
- *Mean Soup* by Betsy Everitt
- *If You're Angry and You Know It* by Cecily Kaiser
- *Andrew's Angry Words* by Dorothea Lachner
- *I Was So Mad* by Norma Simon
- *When I Feel Angry* by Cornelia Maude Spelman
- *Sometimes I'm Bombaloo* by Rachel Vail
- *Alexander and the Terrible, Horrible, No Good, Very Bad Day* by Judith Viorst

Be sure to point out all of the actions or ways in which the characters behave when they are acting on their feelings. Use the following questions to guide your discussion:

- Which character was angry?
- Do you think it was a **good** or **not good** feeling?

- What did the character look like when he or she was angry?
- What did the character do when he or she was angry?
- Did the character use a **Way that Hurts** or a **Way that Helps** to handle his or her anger?

Show and Define Anger

- Use Supplements 4.1 and 4.2 to show children pictures of different examples of angry faces.
- Be sure to point out facial features that depict anger (e.g., furrowed eyebrows, tight lips).

Sample Script

*This is angry. Angry is **not a good** feeling. What does angry look like in this picture? Raise your hand if you've ever felt angry. What did your body look or feel like?*

- Have students share what their bodies felt like when they were angry. Examples include felt hot, had tight muscles, were shaky, or were teary.
- Help the students understand other words similar to anger. Examples include *mad*, *furious*, and *upset*.

Ways of Handling Anger

Introduce the concept of **Ways that Help** and **Ways that Hurt** in handling anger.

Sample Script

Today, we've been talking about a feeling called anger. All people feel angry sometimes, and it's all right to feel angry. Most of the time, something happens to make us angry. This is called a spark. Sparks are little bits of fire that get hotter and hotter and turn into a big angry fire. Just like fire, something "sparks" our anger. There are things we can do to stop anger and keep it from spreading, and there are things we can do that spread the anger and hurt ourselves and others.

Act out the following scenario with Henry:

Henry: "Could I please go to my friend's house and play?"

Teacher: "Not today, Henry. We have to go to the grocery store. Maybe another time."

Discuss or show that when this happened, Henry's muscles got tight, and he began to feel hot. Ask students, "What sparked Henry's anger in this situation? How did his body feel? What do you think Henry did?"

After students have shared their ideas for what Henry did when he was angry, explain that there are two ways that you can deal with your anger: **Ways that Help** and **Ways that Hurt.** Use Supplement 4.3 to introduce **Ways that Help.**

Sample Script

*Henry felt really angry when he couldn't go to his friend's house. Since this happened a long time ago, Henry didn't know about **Ways that Help** and **Ways that Hurt** when handling his anger. In this situation, Henry stuck out his tongue, stomped his feet, and slammed the door to his room. When he was alone in the room, he kicked the wall. This kind of behavior is what I call **Ways that Hurt.** Henry stayed mad and wasn't acting nicely. When he got older and the same thing happened, he knew how to make himself feel better. He learned a special trick called **Stop, Count, In, Out.***

Use Supplements 4.4–4.7 to show students the steps of the **Stop, Count, In, Out** strategy.

	Sample Script
STOP	When you feel a spark, **stop** what you are doing.
COUNT	**Count** to 10.
IN	Take a deep breath **in.**
OUT	Breathe **out.**

*These steps are all **Ways that Help.***

Use the following examples to assess children's understanding of the concept of **Ways that Hurt** and **Ways that Help** in handling anger. Have students stand up if it is a **Way that Helps** and stay sitting if it is a **Way that Hurts.**

Spark	What Henry does	Is it a Way that Helps or a Way that Hurts?
Henry's best friend did not want to share his new toy.	Henry took a deep breath and counted to 10.	It's a Way that Helps.
Henry's mom said he could not watch TV.	Henry yelled, "You're mean!"	It's a Way that Hurts.
Henry's block tower kept falling down before he was done building it.	Henry stopped what he was doing, counted to 10, and took a deep breath in and out.	It's a Way that Helps.
Henry did not get to be first in line when his class went outside for recess.	Henry pushed the line leader out of the way.	It's a Way that Hurts.

1 minute

Closure

Gather your students together, and review the lesson objectives.

Sample Script

*Everyone feels angry sometimes, and there are many ways that we can handle our anger. It is important to use a **Way that Helps** so that we don't hurt ourselves or others.*

10 minutes

Additional Activity

Complete this activity within 2 days of lesson implementation.

Encourage students to cut out and color the stop sign depicted in Supplement 4.8. Have them glue the sign to a wooden craft stick and use it as a reminder to practice the **Stop, Count, In, Out** strategy.

Applying What We Learned

Anticipate

Tell your students to use **Ways that Help** (the **Stop, Count, In, Out** strategy) if something sparks their anger. Prompting them prior to recess, lunch, physical education periods, and partner activities might be particularly helpful.

Remind

If you find that a student is not dealing with his or her anger properly, remind him or her to handle the anger with a **Way that Helps**. Some students might benefit from your modeling the **Stop, Count, In, Out** strategy ("Watch Me." Stop, count, breathe. "Your turn.").

Acknowledge

If you see your students using **Ways that Help** to handle their anger, provide them with specific praise, such as, "I like that you stopped and took a big, deep breath just then. I could tell that something had sparked your anger."

STRONG KIDS™ I'm Angry!

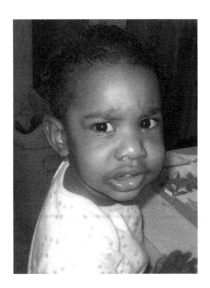

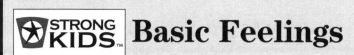 **Basic Feelings**

Angry

Strong Start—Pre-K: A Social and Emotional Learning Curriculum
by Kenneth W. Merrell, Sara A. Whitcomb, and Danielle M. Parisi © 2009 University of Oregon. All rights reserved.

 # The Stop, Count, In, Out Strategy

STOP		When you feel a spark, **stop** what you are doing.
COUNT	1 2 3 4 6 5 9 7 8 10	**Count** to 10.
IN		Take a deep breath **in.**
OUT		Breathe **out.**

STRONG START
LESSON 4

 **STRONG KIDS**™ **The Stop, Count, In, Out Strategy**

Stop

Strong Start—Pre-K: A Social and Emotional Learning Curriculum
by Kenneth W. Merrell, Sara A. Whitcomb, and Danielle M. Parisi © 2009 University of Oregon. All rights reserved.   69

 **STRONG KIDS**™ # The Stop, Count, In, Out Strategy

1

2

4

3

6

5

9

7

8

10

Count

The Stop, Count, In, Out Strategy

In

 **The Stop, Count, In, Out Strategy**

Out

★ STRONG KIDS™ Stop Sign

Strong Start—Pre-K: A Social and Emotional Learning Curriculum
by Kenneth W. Merrell, Sara A. Whitcomb, and Danielle M. Parisi © 2009 University of Oregon. All rights reserved.

73

 **Strong Start Bulletin**

Dear Family,

This week, our **Strong Start** lesson focused on teaching students helpful ways of handling anger. We discussed how our bodies feel when we are angry, and we also listed synonyms for the word **anger**. Throughout the lesson, Henry helped us understand **Ways that Help** and **Ways that Hurt** in dealing with situations that make us angry. We shared ideas about appropriately stopping our **sparks** from turning into big, angry fires. Below is one strategy we practiced:

The Stop, Count, In, Out Strategy

STOP		When you feel a spark, **stop** what you are doing.
COUNT	1 2 3 4 6 5 9 7 8 10	**Count** to 10.
IN		Take a deep breath **in**.
OUT		Breathe **out**.

To better understand handling anger, we read

_____ .

Following are great examples of relevant stories that you may want to read at home:

- *When Sophie Gets Angry—Really, Really Angry* by Molly Bang
- *If You're Angry and You Know It* by Cecily Kaiser
- *Andrew's Angry Words* by Dorothea Lachner
- *Alexander and the Terrible, Horrible, No Good, Very Bad Day* by Judith Viorst

When your child becomes angry at home, remind him or her to:

- Stop and identify the "spark."
- Count to 10, and breathe in and out.
- Act or behave in a **Way that Helps**.

Helping children to choose **Ways that Help** in handling anger is very important. If you see that your child is not making an appropriate choice for handling anger, help him or her to brainstorm a better way. If you notice your child making a great choice, be sure to praise his or her accomplishment (e.g., "I liked the way you took a breath when you started to get angry.").

LESSON 5

When You're Happy

★ **Purpose**

- To teach students to feel happy and to comfort themselves when unhappy

★ **Objectives**

- Students will accurately identify features of people depicting the concept of *happy*.
- Students will describe how their bodies feel when they are happy.
- Students will accurately list synonyms for the word *happy*.
- Students will be exposed to the concept of *Happy Talk*.

MATERIALS NEEDED

- ❑ Henry (stuffed animal mascot)
- ❑ Blank overhead transparency or chart paper
- ❑ Book from the literature list (or one of your choice)
- ❑ Supplement 5.1 (laminated card)
- ❑ Supplement 5.2 (laminated card)
- ❑ Supplement 5.3 (in-class handout)
- ❑ Crayons
- ❑ *Strong Start* Bulletin

2 minutes   # Review

To activate prior knowledge, review and discuss previous topics and main ideas on the concept of *anger*, from Lesson 4. Make sure to provide feedback and refer to the steps of the **Stop, Count, In, Out** strategy.

Sample Script

During our last meeting, we discussed feeling angry. Raise your hand if you can tell me **Ways that Help** *you feel better when you are angry. How about a* **Way that Hurts?**

1 minute   # Introduction

Communicate the lesson's purpose and objectives clearly.

Sample Script

Today, we will talk about feeling happy. Everyone feels happy sometimes. It is a **good** *feeling. Today, we will talk about what happy looks like and what happy feels like. We will think about how we can make ourselves feel happy when we are mad or sad.*

10 minutes   # Read a Book from the Literature List

Read a book from the following list of examples or choose your own book to share with students.

- *Super Completely and Totally the Messiest* by Judith Viorst
- *I Like Me!* by Nancy Carlson
- *The Secret Remedy Book: A Story of Comfort and Love* by Karin Cates
- *Fun is a Feeling* by Chara M. Curtis
- *Today I Feel Silly & Other Moods That Make My Day* by Jamie Lee Curtis
- *A Bad, Bad Day* by Kirsten Hall

As part of your reading, be sure to point out all of the actions or ways in which the characters behave when they are acting on their feelings. Use the following questions to guide your discussion:

- Which character was happy?
- Do you think it was a **good** or **not good** feeling?
- What did the character look like when he or she was happy?
- What did the character do when he or she was happy?

5 minutes # Show and Define Happiness

- Use Supplements 5.1 and 5.2 to show children different examples of happy faces.

    ### Sample Script

    *This is happy. Happy is a **good** feeling. What does happy look like in this picture? Raise your hand if you've ever felt happy. What did your body look or feel like?*

- Point out facial features depicting happy in Supplements 5.1 and 5.2. Orient children toward smiling faces and so forth.

- Have students describe what their bodies felt like when they were happy. Examples include felt comfortable, felt excited, and felt energetic.

- Help children understand words that are similar to *happy*. Examples might include *joy*, *glad*, and *cheerful*.

5 minutes # Happy Talk

Introduce the concept of **Happy Talk.** *Note:* This is a hard concept for young children but may be an important one that they can practice over time.

Sample Script

*Today, we are going to learn about **Happy Talk. Happy Talk** is something that will help us to feel better when we are sad or mad. Remember, it is always okay to feel mad or sad. When we use **Happy Talk,** we can first **Stop, Count, Breathe In, Breathe Out,** and we can then remember that everything is going to be okay.*

Act out the following scene with Henry to model an example and nonexample of Happy Talk.

Scenario 1:

Henry: "Hi. Could I play with your toy?"

Teacher: "Maybe later. I'm taking a turn with it right now."

Henry: "She never shares. I never get to play with her toys."

Scenario 2:

Henry: "Hi. Could I play with your toy?"

Teacher: "Maybe later. I'm taking a turn with it right now."

Henry: [Henry counts to 10 and takes a deep breath.] He uses **Happy Talk** and tells himself and his teacher, "That's okay. I'll get a chance to play with it another time. I'll find something else to do."

Summarize that **Happy Talk** may include working to keep our bodies calm and finding another activity that will make us feel **good** on the inside.

Closure

Gather your students together, and review the lesson objectives.

Sample Script

*Today, we learned about feeling happy and **Happy Talk.** Everyone feels happy. It is a **good** feeling. If we use **Happy Talk,** we can make ourselves feel happy even if we are having **not good** feelings.*

 ## Additional Activity

Complete this activity within 2 days of lesson implementation.

- Provide students with Supplement 5.3 and crayons. Encourage them to draw a picture of their own faces showing happiness. Help children to think about what their mouths, eyes, and eyebrows might look like when they are happy.

- Play Stand Up, Sit Down with students. Use the following examples, and have students stand up if Henry is using **Happy Talk** and sit down if he is not.

Problem	What Henry does	Is he using Happy Talk?
Henry did not get to watch TV before dinner like he usually does.	Henry took a breath. He said, "That's okay. Maybe I can watch TV later."	Yes
Henry wanted to ride his bike. His mom said no.	Henry yelled, "I am never going to ride my bike again!"	No
Henry was hungry for lunch, but his mom had to make it first. Henry had to wait.	Henry took a breath. He said, "That's okay. I'll play with Legos until lunch is ready."	Yes
Henry wanted to play with a friend who lived next door. His friend was not home.	Henry said, "He is not my friend, anyway! I don't ever want to play with him."	No

Applying What We Learned

Anticipate

Help your students to use **Happy Talk** when they are feeling bad. This may be particularly helpful before events that may cause negative feelings, such as partner activities, recess, and choice time.

Remind

If you find a student who is not using **Happy Talk,** tell him or her to take a deep breath and figure out a better way.

Acknowledge

If you are able to observe students using **Happy Talk,** be sure to applaud their application of this complex skill.

STRONG KIDS™ I'm Happy!

Strong Start—Pre-K: A Social and Emotional Learning Curriculum
by Kenneth W. Merrell, Sara A. Whitcomb, and Danielle M. Parisi © 2009 University of Oregon. All rights reserved.

STRONG START
LESSON 5

STRONG KIDS™ | Basic Feelings

Happy

This Is Me When I Am Happy

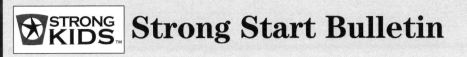

Strong Start Bulletin

Dear Family,

This week, our **Strong Start** lesson focused on teaching students about **happiness.** We discussed how our bodies feel when we are happy and what actions or situations make us feel happy. We also listed synonyms for the word **happy.**

In this lesson, Henry helped us understand **Happy Talk.** We talked about how **Happy Talk** can make us feel better when we are sad or mad. When we use **Happy Talk,** we can stop, count, and take a breath and then remember everything is going to be okay.

To better understand happiness, we read

_____.

Following are great examples of relevant stories that you may want to read at home:
- *Super Completely and Totally the Messiest* by Judith Viorst
- *Fun is a Feeling* by Chara M. Curtis
- *Today I Feel Silly & Other Moods That Make My Day* by Jamie Lee Curtis

When your child becomes sad or mad at home, remind him or her to remember the **Happy Talk** strategy noted above. This can be hard, and your child might need your help to think about a problem in a better way. For example, if your child mistakenly breaks a toy, an example of **Happy Talk** might be, "That's okay. I have other toys," rather than "What will I do? I have nothing to play with now."

Thanks for all of your support in helping your child to be a positive thinker!

LESSON 6

When You're Worried

⭐ Purpose

- To teach students to manage anxiety, worry, and fear

⭐ Objectives

- Students will accurately describe how their bodies feel when they are worried.
- Students will accurately list synonyms for the word *worried.*
- Students will identify situations that might make people worried.
- Students will try a basic relaxation technique.

MATERIALS NEEDED

- ❑ Henry (stuffed animal mascot)
- ❑ Blank overhead transparency or chart paper
- ❑ Book from the literature list (or one of your choice)
- ❑ Supplement 6.1 (laminated card)
- ❑ Supplement 6.2 (laminated card)
- ❑ *Strong Start* Bulletin

2 minutes

Review

To activate prior knowledge, review and discuss previous topics and main ideas from Lesson 5, When You're Happy. Make sure to provide feedback.

Sample Script

*During our last meeting, we learned about **Happy Talk**. Raise your hand if you can tell me an important idea we learned from this lesson.*

1 minute

Introduction

Communicate the lesson's purpose and objectives clearly.

Sample Script

*Today, we will talk about feeling worried. Feeling worried is **not a good** feeling, but everyone feels worried sometimes. It's normal. Feeling worried is sometimes like feeling scared. We will learn how our bodies are when we are worried and think about when we might worry. We will also learn ways to deal with our worries so that we don't feel worried all the time.*

10 minutes

Read a Book from the Literature List

Read a book from the following list of examples or choose your own to share with students.

- *Arthur's Baby* by Marc Brown
- *Will I Have a Friend?* by Miriam Cohen
- *I'm Scared* by Elizabeth Crary
- *Mommy, Don't Go* by Elizabeth Crary
- *Even If I Did Something Awful* by Barbara Shook Hazen
- *Wemberly Worried* by Kevin Henkes
- *The Underbed* by Cathryn Clinton Hoellwarth
- *The Boy Under the Bed* by Preston McClear
- *The Kissing Hand* by Audrey Penn
- *The Good-Bye Book* by Judith Viorst

Be sure to point out all of the actions or ways in which the characters behave when they are acting on their feelings. Use the following questions to guide your discussion:

- Which character was worried?
- Do you think it was a **good** or **not good** feeling?

- What did the character look like when he or she was worried?
- What did the character do when he or she was worried?

Show and Define Worry

- Use Supplement 6.1 to show children different examples of worried faces.

  Sample Script

  *This is worried. Worried can be a **not good** feeling. What does worried look like in this picture? Raise your hand if you've ever felt worried. What did your body look or feel like?*

- Have students share what their bodies feel like when they are worried. Examples include stomachache, shaky hands and bodies, clenched fists, clenched teeth, and tightened muscles.

- Have students show what their bodies look like when they feel worried.

- Help children understand words similar to *worry*. Examples include *bothered, troubled, concerned, nervous,* and *uneasy.*

Letting Go of Worries

Explain to your students that you will be learning about what it is like to be worried and that Henry will help you with this.

Sample Script

Today, we've been talking about feeling worried. When we are worried, we often have a stomachache or maybe our muscles feel tight. When we feel this way, it can be hard to stop ourselves. We think about our worry all of the time. One time Henry felt very worried. His mom was supposed to pick him up from school, but she was not in the school office at the end of the day. Henry's stomach hurt, and he kept thinking, "Where could she be? Where could she be?" How do you think Henry could have comforted himself?

Display Supplement 6.2, and explain how the **Stop, Count, In, Out** strategy and **Happy Talk** can be helpful tools for letting go of worries.

Sample Script

*When you use **Happy Talk**, you can use **Stop, Count, Breathe In, Breathe Out** and then you can remember everything is going to be okay. You can tell your worry to someone you trust. This might help you to remember that this is not the worst problem in the world, and it can be fixed. You might also remember a time when something like this happened before and it turned out okay.*

The Stop, Count, In, Out Strategy

STOP	When you feel a worry, **stop** what you are doing.
COUNT	**Count** to 10.
IN	Take a deep breath **in.**
OUT	Breathe **out.**

Act out the following scenario with Henry.

Henry: "Where could she be? I know my mom is supposed to be here to pick me up!" [Henry takes a deep breath and says to the teacher] "I am worried because my mom is late."

Teacher: "I understand that might make you nervous, but do you remember what happened when your mom was late once before?"

Henry: "Oh, yeah. I got to play with my friends at school for a little longer. It was fun! Mom was just a little late because she had to get gas for her car. She picked me up as soon as she could."

1 minute

Closure

Gather your students together, and review the lesson objectives.

Sample Script

*Today, we talked about feeling worried. Everyone feels worried sometimes, and it does **not** feel **good.** If you're feeling worried, think about **Happy Talk** and the **Stop, Count, In, Out** strategy. Try to comfort yourself and make your body feel calm.*

10 minutes

Additional Activity: Relaxation Exercise

Complete this activity within 2 days of lesson implementation.

Provide students with another strategy for letting go of worries.

Sample Script

Another way to help us let go of our worries is to focus on making our bodies feel better. We are going to practice a special exercise. It might feel silly at first, but if you follow all of my directions, your body will feel more calm.

• Have students find a quiet, comfortable place.

• Ask them to sit or lie quietly. Dim the lights if possible.

• Say, "Close your eyes. Take deep breaths. Breathe in and out slowly."

- Have students tighten their muscles, group by group. Then, ask them to loosen their muscles and make their bodies calm.

- Say, "Think about your favorite place, a place that makes you feel happy and calm."

- Say, "Sit quietly for a few minutes and continue breathing deeply and thinking about your happy place."

Applying What We Learned

Anticipate

Whenever appropriate, remind students to identify times when their bodies may be showing them that they are feeling worried. Prior to situations that may cause worry, such as interruptions in daily routines, remind students to be on the lookout for body clues such as stomachaches, tense muscles, and shaky bodies. Remind them to use the **Stop, Count, In, Out** strategy to help let go of worries.

Remind

If you find a student who is showing physical signs of worry, remind the student to use strategies that will help his or her body to feel calm.

Acknowledge

When you observe students who name their worries or notice students trying to keep a calm body, specify the strategy and compliment them for using it.

STRONG KIDS™ I'm Worried!

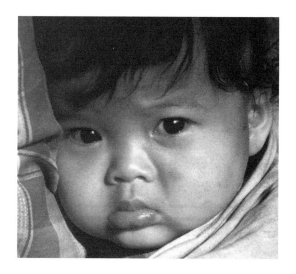

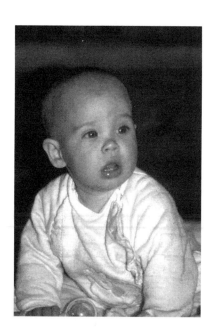

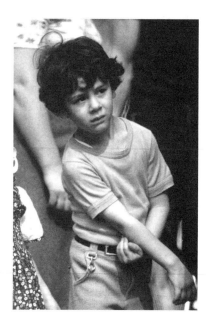

STRONG START
LESSON 6

 **The Stop, Count, In, Out Strategy**

STOP		When you feel a worry, **stop** what you are doing.
COUNT		**Count** to 10.
IN		Take a deep breath **in.**
OUT		Breathe **out.**

Strong Start—Pre-K: A Social and Emotional Learning Curriculum
by Kenneth W. Merrell, Sara A. Whitcomb, and Danielle M. Parisi © 2009 University of Oregon. All rights reserved.

 **Strong Start Bulletin**

Dear Family,

This week, our **Strong Start** lesson focused on teaching students helpful ways of **handling worries.** We discussed how our bodies feel when we are worried, and we also listed synonyms for the word **worry.** Throughout the lesson, Henry helped us understand strategies for letting go of our worries. He taught us to use the **Stop, Count, In, Out strategy** (outlined below) to make us feel better.

The Stop, Count, In, Out Strategy

STOP	STOP	When you feel a worry, **stop** what you are doing.
COUNT	1 2 3 4 6 5 9 7 8 10	**Count** to 10.
IN		Take a deep breath **in.**
OUT		Breathe **out.**

To better understand our worries, we read

_____.

Following are great examples of relevant stories that you may want to read at home:

- *The Kissing Hand* by Audrey Penn
- *The Good-Bye Book* by Judith Viorst
- *Mommy, Don't Go* by Elizabeth Crary
- *I'm Scared* by Elizabeth Crary

When your child becomes worried at home, encourage him or her to let go by using the strategies above and taking time to

1. Name his or her worry.
2. Talk about it.
3. Understand that it is not necessarily the worst problem and can likely be fixed.
4. Think about a time when something like this happened before and turned out okay.

All children worry sometimes, and helping them to understand their worries is important. Thanks for your support in this endeavor!

Strong Start—Pre-K: A Social and Emotional Learning Curriculum
by Kenneth W. Merrell, Sara A. Whitcomb, and Danielle M. Parisi © 2009 University of Oregon. All rights reserved.

LESSON 7

Understanding Other People's Feelings

TEACHER NOTES

★ Purpose

- To teach students how to identify others' feelings

★ Objectives

- Students will learn to use physical cues to understand how someone else is feeling.

MATERIALS NEEDED

- ❑ Henry (stuffed animal mascot)
- ❑ Blank overhead transparency or chart paper
- ❑ Book from the literature list (or one of your choice)
- ❑ Magnifying glass (strongly encouraged)
- ❑ Supplements 7.1–7.6 (feelings pictures of laminated cards)
- ❑ *Strong Start* Bulletin

Review

To activate prior knowledge, review and discuss previous topics and main ideas. Obtain 3–5 adequate ideas from the previous lesson. Make sure to provide feedback.

Sample Script

*During our last meeting, we learned about using the **Stop, Count, In, Out** strategy and **Happy Talk** when we are feeling worried. Raise your hand if you can tell me an important idea we learned from this lesson.*

Introduction

Communicate the lesson's purpose and objectives clearly.

Sample Script

Today, we will learn about understanding how other people feel. To help us understand how other people feel, we will learn how to notice what other people's bodies and faces look like when they are feeling different ways. This will make it easier for us to make friends and solve problems.

Read a Book from the Literature List

Read a book from the following list of examples or choose your own book to share with students.

- *Arthur's Eyes* by Marc Brown
- *Harriet, You'll Drive Me Wild* by Mem Fox
- *Frog in the Middle* by Susanna Gretz
- *Chrysanthemum* by Kevin Henkes
- *Julius: The Baby of the World* by Kevin Henkes
- *The Rat and the Tiger* by Keiko Kasza

Be sure to point out all of the actions or ways in which the characters behave when they are acting on their feelings. Also note when different characters have different feelings in the same situation. Use the following questions to guide your discussion:

- What was one of the feelings the character had?
- Do you think it was a **good** or **not good** feeling?
- What did the character look like when he or she was feeling that way?
- What did the character do when he or she was feeling that way?
- What clues did the character use to help him or her understand how other people were feeling?
- Were there any other times during this story when two people had different feelings in the same situation?

Name and Define Skill

Convey the following main ideas to your students using your own words or the sample script provided.

- It might be possible to tell someone's feelings by looking for visual clues (like a detective).

- It is important to listen to others to find out how they are feeling.

Sample Script

Today, we're going to pretend to be detectives. Detectives are people who use special magnifying glasses to help them see things better and to find clues for solving mysteries. We are going to learn how we can be detectives to figure out how other people are feeling. The first clue we can look at is a person's face. The second clue we can look at is the rest of the person's body.

Modeling

Model some feelings for the class. Begin by showing one of the six basic emotion faces from Supplements 7.1–7.6 and describing how it looks. Then, model and list body language tied to each feeling.

Sample Script

(Show picture of happy face.) *This is happy. A happy face shows a smile.* (Model some happy body clues, e.g., smile, open arms, stand up straight, walk with head high, laugh.) *What body clues show you that I am happy?*

(Show picture of sad face.) *This is sad. A sad face is not smiling. A tear may be rolling down a sad person's cheek.* (Model some sad body clues, e.g., frown, put head down, pull arms close to body, shuffle feet, cry.) *What body clues show you that I am sad?*

Continue by having students identify the remaining faces from Supplements 7.1–7.6. For each feeling, act out the body clues, have students describe what your body looks like, and write down their responses. Examples of body clues include the following:

- *Happy*—smile, open arms, stand up straight, walk with head high, laugh

- *Sad*—frown, put head down, pull arms close to body, shuffle feet, cry

- *Afraid*—open eyes wide, drop head, walk backwards slowly, tremble

- *Angry*—turn red in the face, puff up lips, bare teeth, make threatening eye contact, clench fists, cross arms, take up space (e.g., hold arms away from body), walk quickly, shake

- *Surprised*—open eyes wide, open mouth, step back, put hands on face

- *Disgusted*—stick tongue out, scrunch up eyes and nose, turn head away

Model each feeling again. Have the students guess which feeling you are modeling. Practice with students until they can correctly identify five feelings and tell the clues that helped them to know.

Note: You may need to spend more time on this if the class does not display mastery of interpreting the clues. Consider using student volunteers who can demonstrate mastery to model the feelings.

Closure

Gather your students together, and review the lesson objectives.

Sample Script

Today, we learned about ways we can tell how other people are feeling. We can be detectives and search for clues on others' faces and bodies. Recognizing how others are feeling will help us to be good friends and problem solvers. Be sure to practice your detective skills every day.

Additional Activity: Charades

Complete this activity within 2 days of lesson implementation.

- Work with children in small groups.

- Give each child one of the laminated cards depicting the six basic feelings (Supplements 7.1–7.6).

- One at a time, have the children act out the face and body clues that show the feeling on their card. Have other children take turns at guessing which feeling is being acted out.

Applying What We Learned

Anticipate

Prior to social situations (e.g., partner/group activities, field trips, recess, transition times), remind students to be detectives and use visual clues to try to understand how other people feel.

Remind

If you notice a student is not using clues to understand how other people are feeling, remind him or her to do so. This reminder may be particularly useful in situations requiring problem solving (e.g., arguing over a toy, name-calling, telling on one another).

Acknowledge

If you notice your students using their detective skills and recognizing how other people are feeling, give them praise. Remember to be specific and name the particular skill you observed. For example, if you notice a student comforting another, you might say, "Mikey, I noticed that you used the clues that John was showing to understand how he is feeling. You are a great detective and friend!"

Basic Feelings

Happy

Strong Start—Pre-K: A Social and Emotional Learning Curriculum
by Kenneth W. Merrell, Sara A. Whitcomb, and Danielle M. Parisi © 2009 University of Oregon. All rights reserved.

STRONG START
LESSON 7

⭐ STRONG KIDS™ Basic Feelings

Sad

Strong Start—Pre-K: A Social and Emotional Learning Curriculum
by Kenneth W. Merrell, Sara A. Whitcomb, and Danielle M. Parisi © 2009 University of Oregon. All rights reserved.

99

Basic Feelings

Afraid

Strong Start—Pre-K: A Social and Emotional Learning Curriculum
by Kenneth W. Merrell, Sara A. Whitcomb, and Danielle M. Parisi © 2009 University of Oregon. All rights reserved.

STRONG START
LESSON 7

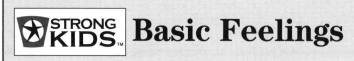

Basic Feelings

Angry

Strong Start—Pre-K: A Social and Emotional Learning Curriculum
by Kenneth W. Merrell, Sara A. Whitcomb, and Danielle M. Parisi © 2009 University of Oregon. All rights reserved.

101

Surprised

Strong Start—Pre-K: A Social and Emotional Learning Curriculum
by Kenneth W. Merrell, Sara A. Whitcomb, and Danielle M. Parisi © 2009 University of Oregon. All rights reserved.

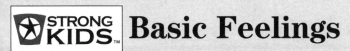

Basic Feelings

Disgusted

Strong Start—Pre-K: A Social and Emotional Learning Curriculum
by Kenneth W. Merrell, Sara A. Whitcomb, and Danielle M. Parisi © 2009 University of Oregon. All rights reserved.   103

 **Strong Start Bulletin**

Dear Family,

This week, our **Strong Start** lesson focused on **how to tell what others are feeling.** We talked about being detectives and searching for clues on others' faces and bodies. Recognizing how others are feeling will help us to be **good friends** and **problem solvers.** We had fun playing charades and guessing what feelings our classmates were modeling.

To better understand other people's feelings, we read

_____ .

Following are great examples of relevant stories that you may want to read at home:

- *Chrysanthemum* by Kevin Henkes

- *Julius: The Baby of the World* by Kevin Henkes

- *Harriet, You'll Drive Me Wild* by Mem Fox

At home, help your child to

1. Be a detective.

2. Look at the body clues of others.

Thanks for all that you do in helping your child to understand the feelings of others. Your support makes a difference in how your child uses the information presented in these lessons!

Strong Start—Pre-K: A Social and Emotional Learning Curriculum
by Kenneth W. Merrell, Sara A. Whitcomb, and Danielle M. Parisi © 2009 University of Oregon. All rights reserved.

LESSON 8

Being a Good Friend

⭐ **Purpose**

- To teach students basic communication and friendship-making skills

⭐ **Objectives**

- Students will discriminate between a *nice voice* and a *not nice voice.*

- Students will practice listening skills.

- Students will learn the importance of eye contact and body language when relating with others.

- Students will learn how to initiate and maintain friendships.

MATERIALS NEEDED

- ❑ Henry (stuffed animal mascot)
- ❑ Blank overhead transparency or chart paper
- ❑ Book from the literature list (or one of your choice)
- ❑ Supplement 8.1 (in-class handout)
- ❑ Drawing paper
- ❑ Crayons
- ❑ *Strong Start* Bulletin

2 minutes Review

To activate prior knowledge, review and discuss previous topics and main ideas. Obtain 1–2 adequate ideas from the previous lesson on understanding others' feelings. Make sure to provide feedback.

Sample Script

During our last meeting, we learned about understanding other people's feelings. Raise your hand if you can tell me an important idea we learned from this lesson.

1 minute Introduction

Communicate the lesson's purpose and objectives clearly.

Sample Script

Today, we will be learning about how to be a good friend. We will learn how to use our words, eyes, ears, and bodies to help us make friends. We will also talk about how to work together with friends.

10 minutes Read a Book from the Literature List

Read a book from the following list of examples or choose your own book to share with students.

- *We Are Best Friends* by Aliki
- *Do You Want to Be My Friend?* by Eric Carle
- *Meet the Barkers: Morgan and Moffat Go to School* by Tomie dePaola
- *Friends* by Helme Heine
- *My Best Friend* by Pat Hutchins
- *Frog and Toad Together* by Arnold Lobel
- *George and Martha* by James Marshall
- *George and Martha One Fine Day* by James Marshall
- *The Best Friends Book* by Todd Parr
- *The Rainbow Fish* by Marcus Pfister
- *The Giving Tree* by Shel Silverstein

Be sure to point out all of the actions or ways in which the characters behave as good friends. Use the following questions to guide your discussion:

- Which people were friends in the story?
- How did they talk to each other?
- How did they become friends?
- What were some of the things they did together?

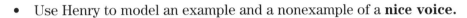

Talking and Listening

- Communicate the necessary body clues for talking nicely, and give examples and nonexamples of a friendly voice.

Sample Script

*Today, we're going to learn about how friends should talk and listen to each other. When we talk to others, we should smile and use a **nice voice**. A **nice voice** is soft and gentle and not loud like yelling.*

- Use Henry to model an example and a nonexample of a **nice voice.**

Nonexample:

Henry: [Yelling and using a **not nice voice**] "Hey! Let me play now!"

Example:

Henry: [Using a **nice voice**] "Hi there. May I play with you?"

- Communicate the necessary body clues for listening, and give examples and nonexamples of being a good listener.

Sample Script

*When friends talk to each other, they use a **nice voice.** Friends are also good listeners. When we listen, we use our eyes, ears, and bodies. We look at the person who is talking, we keep calm bodies, and we hear what the person is saying.*

- Model an example and a nonexample of being a good listener.

Nonexample:

Henry: "Hi there. May I play with you?"

Teacher: [Continues to play and ignores Henry]

Example:

Henry: "Hi there. May I play with you?"

Teacher: [Looking toward Henry, smiles and says] "Sure, Henry. I'd love to have you join in the game!"

Approaching Others and Sharing

Explain how to begin a friendship or an activity with friends. *Note:* It is important to remember that there are cultural differences in social interaction. In some cultures, eye contact may not be an appropriate way to communicate. Please use other more appropriate examples as you see fit.

Sample Script

*When we're friends, we listen to each other and use **nice voices.** Part of being a good friend is noticing others as they come up to you and showing them that you care. When you move close to another and smile and say hi, you're taking notice. When you ask someone to play, you show that you care and want to be a friend. Sometimes it can be hard to know how to join in with others or ask someone to play. Let's make a list of different things we can do or say to show others that we want to be friends.*

 Provide children with examples such as "Hi, do you want to play?" or "Henry, have you ever played with this toy before? Want to give it a try?" Gather further appropriate examples from children.

Explain the importance of maintaining friendships through sharing and working together. Elicit from the students some examples of sharing and working together.

Sample Script

*It is important to always treat our friends in a nice way so that we can stay friends. We should make sure to listen to our friends and use a **nice voice.** It is also important to share and to work together. Sometimes two people will want to use the same thing or play with the same toy. Friends work together, use nice talk, and listen to each other to figure out a way to both be happy.*

Act out the following scenario with Henry:

Henry: "I want to use the purple marker."

Teacher: "That is the one I wanted to use, too. What should we do?"

Henry: "I know. First, you can use it, and when you are finished with it, you can give it to me."

Teacher: "Great idea. Thanks, Henry!"

Closure

1 minute

Gather your students together, and review the lesson objectives.

Sample Script

Today, we learned how to be a good friend. We can use our words, eyes, ears, and bodies to help us make friends. It is also important for us to treat our friends nicely and work together so that we can stay friends.

Additional Activity: Make a Class Book

10 minutes

Complete this activity within 2 days of lesson implementation.

 As a closure activity, have the students each make a page for a class book. Use Supplement 8.1, and ask students to dictate what a good friend does. Then, have them draw pictures. If time permits and students are willing, have a few children share their drawings with the class.

Applying What We Learned

Anticipate

Encourage your students to look and listen to one another and to use **nice voices.** Prompt them prior to social times (e.g., recess, lunch, free play, partner activities). Anticipate situations that might occur within your classroom, and consider acting out scenarios with Henry prior to those situations.

Remind

If you notice a student who is not using his or her friendship skills, remind him or her to listen, to use a **nice voice,** to share, and to work together. It might be necessary at first for you to role-play what these skills look like.

Acknowledge

If you see your students using their friendship skills, be sure to recognize their efforts (e.g., "I like how you asked Mary to play. You used a **nice voice** and had a smile on your face!").

STRONG KIDS™ — What Does a Good Friend Do?

A good friend

_____

_____

_____

_____

_____

Strong Start—Pre-K: A Social and Emotional Learning Curriculum
by Kenneth W. Merrell, Sara A. Whitcomb, and Danielle M. Parisi © 2009 University of Oregon. All rights reserved.

 **Strong Start Bulletin**

Dear Family,

This week, our **Strong Start** lesson focused on how to be a **good friend**. We discussed how friends should talk with a **nice voice** and actively listen to each other by maintaining eye contact, keeping a calm body, and hearing what others have to say. Part of being a good friend also includes noticing others as they approach and showing them that we care. Finally, we talked about how important it is to **share** and **work together** with our friends. The lesson was complete when children compiled a book of words and pictures depicting good friends.

To better understand how to be a good friend, we read

_____.

Following are great examples of relevant stories that you may want to read at home:

- *Frog and Toad Together* by Arnold Lobel
- *The Giving Tree* by Shel Silverstein
- *George and Martha* by James Marshall

At home, help your child to

- Use a **nice voice**
- Use eyes, ears, and bodies to show good listening
- Take notice of others by saying hi or inviting them to play
- Take turns and share

Making and keeping friends can be hard work. Thanks for supporting your child as he or she learns these important skills. Your guidance and acknowledgment will help your child to be a good friend to others.

LESSON 9

TEACHER NOTES

Solving People Problems

⭐ Purpose

- To teach students to solve problems with others

⭐ Objectives

- Students will describe problems that might occur between friends.
- Students will review *Ways that Help* in dealing with anger.
- Students will review *Happy Talk.*
- Students will practice problem-solving strategies.

MATERIALS NEEDED
❑ Henry (stuffed animal mascot)
❑ Blank overhead transparency or chart paper
❑ Book from the literature list (or one of your choice)
❑ Supplement 9.1 (laminated card)
❑ *Strong Start* Bulletin

Review
2 minutes

To activate prior knowledge, review and discuss previous topics and main ideas from Lesson 8, Being a Good Friend. Make sure to provide feedback and refer to the use of nice voices, good listening, and eye contact.

Sample Script

During our last meeting, we discussed how to be a friend. Raise your hand if you can tell me one way that you might be a friend.

Introduction
1 minute

Communicate the lesson's purpose and objectives clearly.

Sample Script

*Today, we will talk about solving problems with others. Everyone has problems sometimes. Problems often happen when we don't agree or when we want to do something that our friends don't. Problems often make us feel mad or sad, and these are **not good** feelings. Today, we will think about how we can make ourselves feel happy when we are mad or sad and how we can solve problems when they happen.*

Read a Book from the Literature List
10 minutes

Read a book from the following list of examples or choose your own book to share with students.

- *Words Are Not for Hurting* by Elizabeth Verdick and Marieka Heinlen
- *Move Over, Twerp* by Martha Alexander
- *I Can't Wait* by Elizabeth Crary
- *I'm Frustrated* by Elizabeth Crary
- *Bet You Can't* by Penny Dale
- *The Knight and the Dragon* by Tomie dePaola
- *Chester's Way* by Kevin Henkes
- *Peter's Chair* by Ezra Jack Keats
- *When Pigasso Met Mootisse* by Nina Laden

Be sure to point out all of the actions or ways in which the characters behave when they are acting on their feelings. Use the following questions to guide your discussion:

- What was one of the feelings the character had?
- Do you think it was a **good** or **not good** feeling?

- What was the problem?

- What did the character do when he or she was faced with a problem?

- How did the character solve his or her problem?

Types of People Problems

Explain the idea of disagreement, or *people problems*, and use Henry to provide an example.

Sample Script

*We have a problem when we can't agree or we want to do something our friends don't. Problems often make us feel sad or mad, and these are **not good** feelings.*

*For example, one time Henry was excited for a playdate at his friend's house because his friend has really cool Legos. When Henry arrived, he had a problem, and it was **not a good** feeling.*

Act out the following scenario with Henry:

Henry: "Hi there. I am so excited for our playdate. I was hoping that we could play with your Legos."

Friend: "Sorry, Henry, but I want to paint with my new paint set."

- Have students share problems they have encountered. Possible examples include arguing over toys, not taking turns, cutting in line, and not working together on a group assignment.

- Ensure respectful sharing by reminding students not to use names and to remember to use nice words.

Review Ways that Help and Happy Talk

Review the concept of **Ways that Help** (Supplement 9.1) for handling anger and using **Happy Talk.**

Sample Script

*When we have a problem, we usually feel mad or sad. It is important for us to remember **Ways that Help** us feel better when we are angry.*

Sample Script

*It is also important to remember **Happy Talk.** Remember, when we use **Happy Talk,** we **Stop, Count, Breathe In, Breathe Out,** and we tell* *ourselves that everything is going to be okay. When we use **Happy Talk,** we can name how we are feeling and tell someone we trust. When we don't use **Happy Talk,** we might get stuck feeling sad or mad.*

---

6 minutes

Comforting Yourself and Solving People Problems

Introduce strategies for solving problems.

- Use the **Stop, Count, In, Out** strategy.
- Use **Happy Talk.**
- Be a friend.
- Make it better.

Sample Script

*When a problem sparks a **not good** feeling, we need to **Stop, Count, In, Out.** After taking a deep breath, we need to continue to comfort ourselves by remembering how to be a friend. When we use **nice voices,** listen, and look at our friends, it will be easier for us to tell them what is wrong and fix the problem. When we work together, we share ideas for fixing the problem so that we both feel better.*

Act out the following scenarios with Henry.

Nonexample of problem solving:

Henry: "I wanted to play with Legos, and I am not going to play with you again if we don't play with Legos."

Friend: [Begins to cry] "Fine. You are not my friend anymore."

The Stop, Count, In, Out Strategy

STOP	When you feel a spark, **stop** what you are doing.
COUNT	**Count** to 10.
IN	Take a deep breath **in.**
OUT	Breathe **out.**

Example of problem solving:

Henry: [Uses the **Stop, Count, In, Out** strategy] "Hmm. I really wanted to play with Legos, and you want to paint. That makes me feel a little mad on the inside."

Friend: "Maybe we could make it better. We could ask my mom to help fix the problem, or we could decide to play something else."

Henry: "I know! First, we could paint, and then we could play with Legos!"

Friend: "Great idea, Henry!"

Make sure children understand the difference between the scenarios, and encourage them to remember to use strategies for fixing problems.

Sample Script

There are many different ways for friends to fix problems. When Henry and his friend wanted to do two different things, they came up with many ideas for solving the problem. They thought about picking a whole new activity, painting first and then playing with Legos, playing with Legos first and then painting, asking an adult for help, or deciding to play together on another day. They decided to paint pictures for a while and then switch to playing with Legos so that they both got to do what they wanted. When you think of ideas with your friends, remember there are many ways to solve the problem.

Closure

Gather your students together, and review the lesson objectives.

Sample Script

*Today, we learned about fixing problems we have with others. Everyone has problems sometimes, and these problems often make us have not good feelings. We can use the **Stop, Count, In, Out** strategy and **Happy Talk** to solve problems with others.*

Additional Activity: Role Play

Complete this activity within 2 days of lesson implementation.

To help your students build fluency in solving people problems, use Henry to act out more nonexamples of problem solving similar to the one provided in the lesson. After you have acted out the nonexample, have students come up and act out how they might fix the problem. Be sure to praise students' efforts to use **Ways that Help** and **Happy Talk.** Try to use scenarios that are relevant to daily situations that arise in your classroom. Example scenarios are provided in the chart on page 118. Use topics such as sharing, cleaning up, following rules during a game, and choosing a friend to sit next to.

Problem	What happens	Making it better
Henry wants a turn on the swings, but they are all being used.	Henry yells loudly at you, "It's my turn!"	Henry takes a deep breath and says to you, "Could I have a turn in a few minutes?"
You and Henry are playing with blocks, and it is clean-up time.	Henry walks away and does not help you clean up.	You take a breath and use a nice voice to say, "Henry, you played this game with me. Will you help me clean up?"
You and Henry are coloring. You both want to use the green crayon.	You and Henry both grab at the crayon and yell, "It's mine!"	You decide to let Henry use it first and choose a different part of the picture to work on. Henry gives you the green crayon when he is done with it.

Applying What We Learned

Anticipate

Encourage your students to be problem solvers when they disagree with one another. Remind them to use the **Stop, Count, In, Out** strategy and **Happy Talk** when a problem arises. Be sure to prompt them prior to events during which problems might arise (e.g., a difficult board game, a game with a lot of rules, a group project).

Remind

If you notice a student who is not problem-solving, remind him or her to use the strategies learned in class. You might have to break the problem-solving process into manageable parts. For example, first encourage the student to engage in the **Stop, Count, In, Out** strategy, and then prompt him or her to use **Happy Talk** and be a friend in order to help solve the problem.

Acknowledge

If you see your students problem-solving, be sure to give specific praise (e.g., "I really liked that you stopped and took a breath and then decided to take turns with that game. Great problem solving!").

 # The Stop, Count, In, Out Strategy

STOP		When you feel a spark, **stop** what you are doing.
COUNT		**Count** to 10.
IN		Take a deep breath **in.**
OUT		Breathe **out.**

119

 **Strong Start Bulletin**

Dear Family,

This week, our **Strong Start** lesson focused on how to **solve problems** with others. We brainstormed a list of potential problems we might have with our peers. Then, we talked about the actions we might take when problems arise. We learned that we could use the **Stop, Count, In, Out breathing strategy** when we get angry, and after taking a deep breath, we could comfort ourselves by remembering how to be a friend. When we use nice voices, listen, and look at friends, it will be easier to work together and share ideas for fixing the problem so that we all feel better. We practiced our **problem-solving skills** by role-playing with classmates. The following table reflects an example of problem-solving behavior.

Problem	What Henry does after Stop, Count, In, Out	Is he problem-solving or not problem-solving?
Henry wants to play with Legos, but his friend wants to paint.	Henry and his friend decide to paint for a while and then play Legos.	He is problem-solving.
Henry wants to play with Legos, but his friend wants to paint.	Henry does not listen to his friend's ideas and says, "I'm not going to play with you anymore."	He is not problem-solving.

To better understand how to solve people problems, we read

_____ .

Following are great examples of relevant stories that you may want to read at home:
- _Chester's Way_ by Kevin Henkes
- _I'm Frustrated_ by Elizabeth Crary
- _I Can't Wait_ by Elizabeth Crary

When problems arise at home, help your child to
- Stop and take a deep breath
- Be a friend by looking and listening to others
- Work with others to brainstorm a solution

If you see your child problem-solving, be sure to congratulate his or her efforts (e.g., "I really liked that you stopped and took a breath and then decided to take turns with that game. Great problem solving!"). Thanks again for your support!

Strong Start—Pre-K: A Social and Emotional Learning Curriculum
by Kenneth W. Merrell, Sara A. Whitcomb, and Danielle M. Parisi © 2009 University of Oregon. All rights reserved.

LESSON 10

TEACHER NOTES

_____

_____

_____

_____

_____

_____

_____

_____

_____

_____

_____

_____

_____

_____

_____

_____

_____

_____

_____

_____

Finishing UP!

⭐ Purpose

- To review the major concepts and skills in the *Strong Start—Pre-K* curriculum

⭐ Objectives

- Students will review the purpose of the *Strong Start—Pre-K* curriculum.

- Students will name feelings and describe *okay* and *not okay* ways of expressing feelings.

- Students will review *Happy Talk* and the *Stop, Count, In, Out* strategy.

MATERIALS NEEDED

- ❑ Henry (stuffed animal mascot)
- ❑ Blank overhead transparency or chart paper
- ❑ Supplement 10.1 (laminated card)
- ❑ Supplement 10.2 (laminated card)
- ❑ Supplement 10.3 (laminated card)
- ❑ Book from the literature list (or one of your choice)
- ❑ *Strong Start* Bulletin

Preparation

The Finishing UP! lesson consists of a review of the major concepts presented in this curriculum. It may be helpful to review previous lessons prior to presenting this lesson. Although this lesson is designed to be taught during one time period of approximately 25 minutes, it may be extended into two separate lessons at your discretion and depending on the needs of your children. Following is an outline of topics covered.

Review of Topics

Understanding Your Feelings 1 and 2

- Supplement 10.1 of the six basic feelings.
- Identified feelings as those that feel **good** and **not good** on the inside.
- Identified **okay** and **not okay** ways of showing feelings.

When You're Angry

- Supplement 10.2, which shows the **Stop, Count, In, Out** strategy.
- Identified how our bodies feel when we are angry.
- Identified synonyms for *anger*.
- Identified situations when we might feel angry.
- Reviewed **Ways that Help** and **Ways that Hurt** in handling anger.

When You're Happy

- Identified how our bodies feel when we are happy.
- Identified synonyms for *happy*.
- Learned concept of **Happy Talk.**

When You're Worried

- Identified how our bodies feel when we are worried.
- Identified synonyms for the word *worry*.
- Identified how **Happy Talk** and the **Stop, Count, In, Out** strategy can help us when we are worried.
- Learned relaxation strategy for keeping a calm body.

Understanding Other People's Feelings

- Supplement 10.1 of the six basic feelings.
- Identified physical cues to understand how someone else is feeling.

Being a Good Friend

- Identified **nice voices** and **not nice voices.**

- Identified listening skills: eye contact and body language.

- Learned about making and keeping friends.

Solving People Problems

- Reviewed the **Stop, Count, In, Out** strategy.

- Reviewed **Happy Talk.**

- Reviewed how to be a friend.

- Identified how to fix problems.

Introduction

10 minutes

Communicate the lesson's purpose and objectives clearly. Explain to students that they will complete the final lesson of the *Strong Start* curriculum. Tell them that topics they have been covering for the past few weeks will be reviewed. Point out that they have learned many skills during this unit that are vital to their social and emotional health, and they will have opportunities to use these skills throughout their lives.

Sample Script

Today, we are going to complete a special class called Strong Start. In this class, we learned with a special friend. His name is Henry. In this class, Henry helped us understand our feelings and other people's feelings. He also helped us learn about being a good friend. He is a special part of our class. Even though this is our last lesson, Henry will continue to be with us. Every time we met over the last several weeks, we did special exercises. We didn't run outside or lift big, heavy weights. During the Feelings Exercise Group, we worked on growing strong on the inside instead of on the outside. Everyone needs to be healthy—on the inside and on the outside. This class helped us to be healthy on the inside and in the way we work and play with other people.

Use Supplement 10.3 to review the topics covered in *Strong Start.*

Sample Script

Show me your hand if you can tell me some of the important things we learned in this class.

Point to the picture cues on Supplement 10.3 to review the following lesson topics:

- Understanding our feelings

- Understanding other people's feelings

- Feeling angry
- Feeling happy
- Feeling worried
- Being a friend
- Solving people problems

Read a Book from the Literature List

Read a book from the following list of examples or choose your own book to share with students. Think about choosing a book that will allow you to point out several of the skills learned during *Strong Start*. Use this portion of the lesson as an opportunity to discuss any terms or concepts that may be relevant to your class at this time, to revisit any of the ideas that need expansion, or to simplify and refresh ideas.

- *Feelings* by Aliki
- *The Way I Feel* by Janan Cain
- *Today I Feel Silly & Other Moods That Make My Day* by Jamie Lee Curtis
- *Feelings* by Joanne Brisson Murphy
- *The Feelings Book* by Todd Parr
- *My Many Colored Days* by Dr. Seuss

Closure

Gather your students together, and review key points.

Sample Script

Today, we reviewed many things we have learned in Strong Start. We learned about our feelings and other people's feelings. We learned how to be a good friend and how to solve problems with others. Henry has been our very good friend and he has taught us so much. Now that we have completed our lessons, we need to continue to work hard to remember all that Henry has shared with us. He will continue to be a part of our classroom community and remind us of all that we have learned.

Congratulations! You have completed Strong Start and have learned how to be strong on the inside and in the way that you work and play with other people.

 **STRONG KIDS™** # Basic Feelings

Happy

Sad

Afraid

Angry

Surprised

Disgusted

The Stop, Count, In, Out Strategy

STOP		When you feel a spark, **stop** what you are doing.
COUNT	1 2 3 4 6 5 9 7 8 10	**Count** to 10.
IN		Take a deep breath **in.**
OUT		Breathe **out.**

Strong Start—Pre-K: A Social and Emotional Learning Curriculum
by Kenneth W. Merrell, Sara A. Whitcomb, and Danielle M. Parisi © 2009 University of Oregon. All rights reserved.

 **About Strong Start**

We will learn about our feelings.

feeling *angry*   feeling *happy*   feeling *worried*

We will learn about other people's feelings.

We will learn about being a friend.

We will learn about solving problems.

And we will learn how to relax and feel calm.

Strong Start Bulletin

Dear Family,

Today, your child participated in the last lesson of **Strong Start,** a curriculum designed to boost the social and emotional development of young children. In this class, we learned with a special stuffed bear, **Henry.** Henry helped us understand our feelings and other people's feelings. He also helped us learn about being a good friend. He is a special part of our class. Even though this was our last lesson, Henry will continue to be with us in class and serve as a reminder of all that we have learned. During our lessons over the last several weeks, we engaged in activities and discussions that will encourage your child to work on being **healthy** on the inside as well as the outside.

Strong Start helped your child

Learn about our feelings

Learn about other people's feelings

Learn about being a friend

Learn about solving problems

And learn how to relax and feel calm

Although the lessons of **Strong Start** have been completed, please continue to encourage your child to use the skills and strategies presented in class and in the bulletins sent home. Together, we can continue to support your child's social and emotional health. Thank you!

Strong Start—Pre-K: A Social and Emotional Learning Curriculum
by Kenneth W. Merrell, Sara A. Whitcomb, and Danielle M. Parisi © 2009 University of Oregon. All rights reserved.

Appendices

Strong Start
Booster Lesson 1

**TEACHER
NOTES**

_____

_____

_____

_____

_____

_____

_____

_____

_____

_____

_____

_____

_____

_____

_____

_____

_____

_____

⭐ Purpose

- To review *Strong Start—Pre-K* Lessons 1–6

⭐ Objectives

- Students will review the purpose of the *Strong Start—Pre-K* curriculum.

- Students will name feelings and describe *okay* and *not okay* ways of expressing feelings.

- Students will review *Happy Talk* and the *Stop, Count, In, Out* strategy.

MATERIALS NEEDED

- ❑ Henry (stuffed animal mascot)
- ❑ Blank overhead transparency or chart paper
- ❑ Supplement 1.1 (laminated card)
- ❑ Book from the literature list in Appendix C (or one of your choice)
- ❑ Supplements 2.1–2.6 (feelings pictures on laminated cards)
- ❑ Supplement 4.3 (laminated card)
- ❑ An envelope for each student
- ❑ Supplement A.1 (bingo card, one for each student)
- ❑ Supplement A.2 (cutout feelings pictures, six per student)
- ❑ Supplement A.3 (bingo spinner)
- ❑ Bingo markers
- ❑ Paper plates, brads, scissors, and crayons

Preparation

The first booster lesson consists of a review of the major concepts presented in Lessons 1–6 of this curriculum. It may be helpful to flip back through these lessons prior to presenting this lesson. This might also be an appropriate time to focus on content that students have not yet mastered. Be sure to choose a book from the literature list (Appendix C) that addresses the needs of your class.

1 minute

Introduction

Communicate the lesson's purpose and objectives clearly. Explain to your students that topics from the *Strong Start* curriculum will be reviewed. Tell them that it is always important to review the many skills previously introduced because they are vital to social and emotional health, and students will have opportunities to use these skills throughout their lives. Use Supplement 1.1 (from Lesson 1).

Sample Script

Today, we are going to take time to remember a special class called Strong Start. In this class, we learned with a special friend. Henry has been with us since we began Strong Start, and he has helped us to understand our feelings and other people's feelings. He has also helped us to learn about being a good friend. He is a special part of our class. Each week, when we participated in Strong Start lessons, we completed special exercises. We didn't run outside or lift big, heavy weights. We worked on growing strong on the inside during the Feelings Exercise Group. Everyone needs to be healthy—on the inside and on the outside. This class helped us to learn how to be healthy on the inside for our whole lives.

10 minutes

Read a Book from the Literature List

Choose a book from the literature list (Appendix C) that includes concepts relevant to your class at this time. Use the book as a forum for further discussion. Consider how characters in the story are feeling, how they handle their feelings, or how they recognize the feelings of others.

15 minutes

Review of Topics

Explain that a large part of *Strong Start* had to do with naming feelings and handling our feelings. Use the following script as a guide for your discussion.

Sample Script

The lessons that we learned a long time ago included giving names to our feelings. It is important to know how to name our feelings because it helps us to tell others how we are feeling on the inside. When we can tell others how we are feeling, it may seem easier to be good friends and to solve problems.

Use the following ideas and activities to further your discussion.

1. Understanding your feelings

   • Display and review Supplements 2.1–2.6 (from Lesson 2) of the six basic feelings.

   • Remind students that it is okay to have any feeling and that many people will have different feelings in the same situation. This is also an appropriate time to discuss that some people might be feeling more than one feeling at once (e.g., I was surprised and happy when I arrived at my surprise birthday party).

   • Consider engaging in an activity at a later time that allows students to label feelings and determine which are **good** and **not good** feelings. Examples of activities frequently used are included in the Additional Activities section. Encourage students to give synonyms for various feelings and to identify how their bodies feel when they are experiencing an emotion.

2. **Okay** and **not okay** ways to handle feelings

   • Remind students that there are **okay** and **not okay** ways of showing feelings.

3. Angry

   • Display Supplement 4.3 (from Lesson 4), The **Stop, Count, In, Out** strategy.

   • Identify situations when we might feel angry.

   • Play Stand Up, Sit Down with the following examples to remind children of **Ways that Help** and **Ways that Hurt** in handling anger.

Spark	What Henry does	Is it a Way that Helps or a Way that Hurts?
Henry's friends say that he can't play in the dramatic play area.	Henry yells, "I'll never be your friend again!"	It's a Way that Hurts.
Henry's friends say that he can't play in the dramatic play area.	Henry takes a deep breath and counts to 10 before asking the teacher for help.	It's a Way that Helps.

4. Happy

   • Remind children about the concept of **Happy Talk.**

   • Play Stand Up, Sit Down with the following examples to help students review **Happy Talk.**

Problem	What Henry says to himself	Is Henry using Happy Talk?
Henry's friends say that he can't play in the dramatic play area.	They never let me play! I'll never play with them again.	No
Henry's friends say that he can't play in the dramatic play area.	I am mad, and I think I need the teacher to help me fix this.	Yes

5. Worry

- Review how **Happy Talk** and the **Stop, Count, In, Out** strategy can help us when we are worried.

- Review how to keep a calm body.

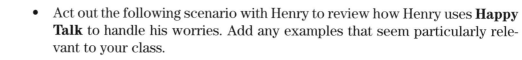

- Act out the following scenario with Henry to review how Henry uses **Happy Talk** to handle his worries. Add any examples that seem particularly relevant to your class.

Henry: "My teacher is not here today because she is sick. There is a new teacher. What if she doesn't know the rules? What if she forgets to hand out snack? What if she doesn't know that we don't turn all the lights off at rest time?"

Henry: [Henry counts to 10 and takes a deep breath. He approaches the substitute teacher.] "I am a little scared because my teacher is not here today and maybe you don't know how things work."

Substitute teacher: "Well, Henry. Thanks for being brave and naming your feeling. Maybe you can help me remember how things are supposed to go?"

Closure

1 minute

Gather your students together, and review key points.

Sample Script

*Today, we reviewed much of what we learned in Strong Start. We reviewed how to label our feelings, and we discussed **okay** and **not okay** ways to handle our feelings. Henry has helped us to remember these important skills, and he will continue to do so. Next time we meet, we will talk more about being a good friend and solving problems with others.*

10 minutes **Additional Activities**

Complete one or more of these activities within 2 days of lesson implementation.

Paper Plate Faces—Have students decorate paper plates that look like themselves. Give students brads, and have them fasten smiles, frowns, and so forth to the mouth portion. Ask students to practice using the paper plate to show different feelings.

Feelings Envelope—Have students cut the six basic feelings from Supplement A.2 and place them in an envelope. Have them pull out the feeling they are experiencing.

Feelings Bingo—Use the bingo cards (Supplements A.1) to play a developmentally appropriate game of bingo. In preparation for bingo, use Supplement A.3 to create a bingo spinner. Fasten the spinner arrow to the center of the circle with a brad. Encourage children to take turns using the bingo spinner. Have children place a marker on the feeling on their bingo board that matches the feeling the spinner is pointing to. Have children try to cover their entire boards with markers.

 **Strong Start Feelings Bingo**

STRONG KIDS™ Basic Feelings Cards

Strong Start—Pre-K: A Social and Emotional Learning Curriculum
by Kenneth W. Merrell, Sara A. Whitcomb, and Danielle M. Parisi © 2009 University of Oregon. All rights reserved.

Bingo Spinner

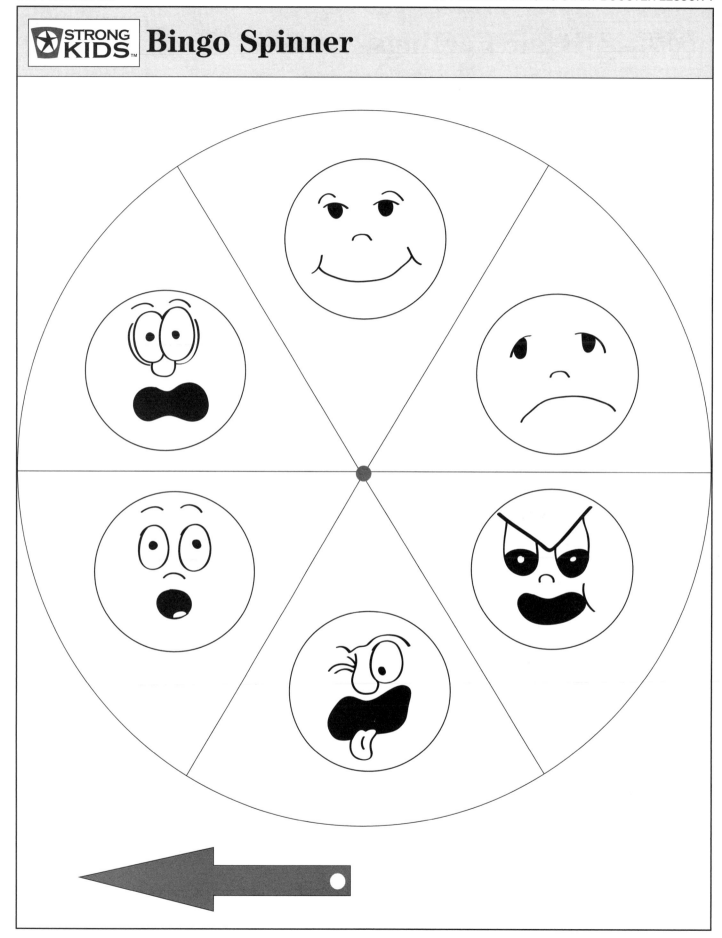

Strong Start—Pre-K: A Social and Emotional Learning Curriculum
by Kenneth W. Merrell, Sara A. Whitcomb, and Danielle M. Parisi © 2009 University of Oregon. All rights reserved.

Strong Start
Booster Lesson 2

TEACHER
NOTES

_____

_____

_____

_____

_____

_____

_____

_____

_____

_____

_____

_____

_____

_____

_____

_____

_____

_____

_____

⭐ Purpose

- To review *Strong Start—Pre-K* Lessons 7–9

⭐ Objectives

- Students will review how to use physical cues to understand how someone else is feeling.

- Students will review the concept that different people have different feelings in the same situation.

- Students will review how good friends use eyes, ears, and bodies to show caring.

- Students will review problem-solving strategies.

MATERIALS NEEDED

- ❏ Henry (stuffed animal mascot)
- ❏ Blank overhead transparency or chart paper
- ❏ Supplements 7.1–7.6 (feelings pictures on laminated cards)
- ❏ Book from the literature list in Appendix C (or one of your choice)
- ❏ Supplement 9.1 (laminated card)
- ❏ Class Book developed during Lesson 8 (Being a Good Friend)

Preparation

The second booster lesson consists of a review of the major concepts presented in Lessons 7–9 of this curriculum. It may be helpful to flip back through these lessons prior to presenting this lesson. This might also be an appropriate time to focus on content that students have not yet mastered. Be sure to choose a book from the literature list that addresses the needs of your class.

Introduction

Communicate the lesson's purpose and objectives clearly. Explain to your students that topics from the *Strong Start* curriculum will be reviewed. Remind your students that it is always important to review the many skills previously introduced because they are vital to social and emotional health, and students will have opportunities to use these skills throughout their lives.

To activate prior knowledge, review and discuss topics and main ideas from the previous booster lesson. Make sure to refer to naming feelings and identifying those that are **good** and **not good.** Have students give examples of **okay** and **not okay** ways of showing feelings. Use Supplements 7.1–7.6 (from Lesson 7).

Sample Script

During our last meeting, we discussed how to name our feelings. We talked about what our bodies look like when we are experiencing a feeling and what we do to handle our feelings. Raise your hand if you can tell me an important idea we learned during that lesson.

Today, we are going to continue to remember a special class called Strong Start. Henry will be with us and will help us to remember how to understand other people's feelings and how to be a good friend.

Read a Book from the Literature List

Choose a book from the literature list (Appendix C) that includes concepts relevant to your class at this time. Use the book as a forum for further discussion. Consider how characters in the story are feeling, how they handle their feelings, or how they recognize the feelings of others.

Review of Topics

Explain that a large part of *Strong Start* had to do with looking at the faces and bodies of others to understand how they are feeling. Another important part of *Strong Start* included thinking about how we use our bodies to show that we are good friends and problem solvers.

Sample Script

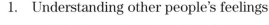

The lessons that we learned a long time ago helped us to be detectives and search for clues to help us figure out how other people are feeling. We learned to pay attention to the faces and bodies of the people around us. Being detectives makes it easier for us to make friends and solve problems.

Use the following ideas and activities to further your discussion.

1. Understanding other people's feelings

   - Display and review Supplements 7.1–7.6 (from Lesson 7) of the six basic feelings.

   - Remind students that it is okay to have any feeling and that many people will have different feelings in the same situation.

   - Use the examples of Henry's feelings (in the chart below) to help children better understand how different children may have different feelings in the same situation.

2. Being a good friend

   - Remind students that good friends use **nice voices** and use eyes, ears, and calm bodies when listening to others.

   - Review how good friends take notice and care. Consider engaging in the additional activity presented at the end of this lesson.

Situation	How Henry looks and feels
During recess, Henry's teacher tells the class that they are going to learn a new game.	Henry smiles and jumps up and down. He is *happy* because he loves new games.
Fish sticks are served for lunch at school.	Henry turns his head away and scrunches up his nose. He is *disgusted* because he does not like to eat fish sticks.
The wind is blowing, and there is a loud crack of thunder.	Henry jumps and then hides his head under his pillow. He is *afraid.*
Henry's best friend is going to a new school.	Henry hangs his head, and a tear drips from his eye. He is *sad* that his friend is leaving.
Henry walks in the front door and finds his mom has baked cookies.	He smiles and runs to his mom and says, "I didn't know you were making cookies today!" He is *surprised.*
Henry's baby sister chewed on his favorite toy.	Henry turns red in the face and clenches his fists. He is *angry.*

3. Solving people problems

- Review strategies for solving problems. Remind students to use a **Way that Helps** in handling anger and **Happy Talk.**

- Review the following concepts that help when trying to make a problem better.

  Use the **Stop, Count, In, Out** strategy (Supplement 9.1 from Lesson 9).

  Use **Happy Talk.**

  Be a friend.

  Make it better.

  Emphasize that solving problems involves helping all parties to feel better.

- Engage in a sharing activity. Have students think about times when they have had problems (e.g., arguing over toys, not taking turns, working together). Encourage students to consider whether or not they effectively problem-solved the situation.

- Ensure respectful sharing by reminding students not to use names and to remember to use nice words.

1 minute

Closure

Gather your students together, and review key points.

Sample Script

Today, we reviewed much of what we learned in Strong Start. We reviewed how to be detectives and look for body clues so that we know how others are feeling. We remembered how to be good friends and problem solvers. Henry has helped us to remember these important skills. He has been our very good friend and has taught us so much. Now that we have completed our review lessons, we need to continue to work hard to remember all that Henry has shared with us. He will continue to be a part of our classroom community and remind us of all that we have learned.

10 minutes

Additional Activity: Class Book

Complete this activity within 2 days of lesson implementation.

If your class compiled a class book during Lesson 8 (Supplement 8.1), pull out the book, and read it aloud to the class. Consider adding new ideas based on what children have learned over time.

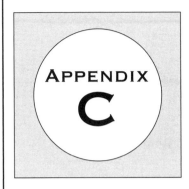

Recommended *Strong Start—Pre-K* Literature List

APPENDIX C

Lesson 1: The Feelings Exercise Group

- *Feelings* by Aliki
- *The Way I Feel* by Janan Cain
- *Feelings* by Joanne Brisson Murphy
- *The Feelings Book* by Todd Parr
- *My Many Colored Days* by Dr. Seuss

Lesson 2: Understanding Your Feelings 1

- *My First Day of Nursery School* by Becky Edwards
- *Feelings* by Aliki
- *Everybody Has Feelings or Todos Tenemos Sentimientos* by Charles E. Avery
- *How Are You Peeling? Foods with Moods* by Saxton Freymann and Joost Elffers
- *On Monday When It Rained* by Cherryl Kachenmeister
- *Feelings* by Joanne Brisson Murphy
- *The Feelings Book* by Todd Parr
- *Lots of Feelings* by Shelley Rotner

Lesson 3: Understanding Your Feelings 2

- *The Chocolate-Covered-Cookie Tantrum* by Deborah Blumenthal
- *Today I Feel Silly & Other Moods That Make My Day* by Jamie Lee Curtis
- *The Grumpy Morning* by Pamela Duncan Edwards
- *Chrysanthemum* by Kevin Henkes
- *Julius: The Baby of the World* by Kevin Henkes
- *Bye, Bye!* by Nancy Kaufmann
- *The Kissing Hand* by Audrey Penn
- *Sometimes I Like to Cry* by Elizabeth and Henry Stanton

Lesson 4: When You're Angry

- *The Cranky Day and Other Thomas the Tank Engine Stories* by W. Awdry
- *When Sophie Gets Angry—Really, Really Angry* by Molly Bang
- *The Chocolate-Covered-Cookie Tantrum* by Deborah Blumenthal
- *Feeling Angry* by Althea Braithwaite
- *Mean Soup* by Betsy Everitt
- *If You're Angry and You Know It* by Cecily Kaiser
- *Andrew's Angry Words* by Dorothea Lachner
- *I Was So Mad* by Norma Simon
- *When I Feel Angry* by Cornelia Maude Spelman
- *Sometimes I'm Bombaloo* by Rachel Vail
- *Alexander and the Terrible, Horrible, No Good, Very Bad Day* by Judith Viorst

Lesson 5: When You're Happy

- *Super Completely and Totally the Messiest* by Judith Viorst
- *I Like Me!* by Nancy Carlson
- *The Secret Remedy Book: A Story of Comfort and Love* by Karin Cates
- *Fun is a Feeling* by Chara M. Curtis
- *Today I Feel Silly & Other Moods That Make My Day* by Jamie Lee Curtis
- *A Bad, Bad Day* by Kristen Hall

Lesson 6: When You're Worried

- *Arthur's Baby* by Marc Brown
- *Will I Have a Friend?* by Miriam Cohen
- *I'm Scared* by Elizabeth Crary
- *Mommy, Don't Go* by Elizabeth Crary
- *Even If I Did Something Awful* by Barbara Shook Hazen
- *Wemberly Worried* by Kevin Henkes
- *The Underbed* by Cathryn Clinton Hoellwarth
- *The Boy Under the Bed* by Preston McClear
- *The Kissing Hand* by Audrey Penn
- *The Good-Bye Book* by Judith Viorst

Lesson 7:
Understanding Other People's Feelings

- *Arthur's Eyes* by Marc Brown
- *Harriet, You'll Drive Me Wild* by Mem Fox
- *Frog in the Middle* by Susanna Gretz
- *Chrysanthemum* by Kevin Henkes
- *Julius: The Baby of the World* by Kevin Henkes
- *The Rat and the Tiger* by Keiko Kasza

Lesson 8: Being a Good Friend

- *We Are Best Friends* by Aliki
- *Do You Want to Be My Friend?* by Eric Carle
- *Meet the Barkers: Morgan and Moffat Go to School* by Tomie dePaola
- *Friends* by Helme Heine
- *My Best Friend* by Pat Hutchins
- *Frog and Toad Together* by Arnold Lobel
- *George and Martha* by James Marshall
- *George and Martha One Fine Day* by James Marshall
- *The Best Friends Book* by Todd Parr
- *The Rainbow Fish* by Marcus Pfister
- *The Giving Tree* by Shel Silverstein

Lesson 9: Solving People Problems

- *Words Are Not for Hurting* by Elizabeth Verdick and Marieka Heinlen
- *Move Over, Twerp* by Martha Alexander
- *I Can't Wait* by Elizabeth Crary
- *I'm Frustrated* by Elizabeth Crary
- *Bet You Can't* by Penny Dale
- *The Knight and the Dragon* by Tomie dePaola
- *Chester's Way* by Kevin Henkes
- *Peter's Chair* by Ezra Jack Keats
- *When Pigasso Met Mootisse* by Nina Laden

Lesson 10: Finishing UP!

- *Feelings* by Aliki
- *The Way I Feel* by Janan Cain
- *Today I Feel Silly & Other Moods That Make My Day* by Jamie Lee Curtis
- *Feelings* by Joanne Brisson Murphy
- *The Feelings Book* by Todd Parr
- *My Many Colored Days* by Dr. Seuss